September Tide

a play

Daphne du Maurier

Revised version by Mark Rayment

D0838975

Samuel French

www.samuelfrench-london.co.uk
www.samuelfrench.com (US)

ISBN 978 0 573 01905 0

Please see page iv for further copyright information

SEPTEMBER TIDE

First performed at the Aldwych Theatre, London, on 15th December, 1948, with the following cast:

Robert Hanson	Cyril Raymond
Mrs Tucket	Dandy Nichols
Cherry Davies	Anne Leon
Evan Davies	Michael Gough
Stella Martyn	Gertrude Lawrence
Jimmy Martyn	Bryan Forbes

Directed by Irene Hentschel
Designed by Michael Relph

This revised version opened at the King's Head Theatre, London, on 20th July 1993 with the following cast:

Robert Hanson	Peter Byrne
Mrs Tucket	Mary Chester
Cherry Davies	Francesca Hunt
Evan Davies	Brendan Coyle
Stella Martyn	Susannah York
Jimmy Martyn	Toby Walton

Directed by Mark Rayment
Designed by Jonathan Fensom

COPYRIGHT INFORMATION

(See also page ii)

CHARACTERS

Robert Hanson, a friend of the family
Mrs Tucket, the daily woman
Cherry Davies
Evan Davies, Cherry's husband
Stella Martyn, Cherry's mother
Jimmy Martyn, Stella's son

ACT I
SCENE 1

The living-room of Stella Martyn's house on a Cornish estuary. Late afternoon, summer 1948

The furniture — sofa, piano, armchairs, tables, stove, etc. — suggest the interior of a simple but comfortable seaside home. A low doorway and semi-visible curved stairwell, UC, *give the impression of a studio above the main stage. A door, extreme* L, *leads off to the kitchen, pantry and the rear of the house. Another door, extreme* R, *leads to the front door and the main staircase. The house is directly above the harbour. Throughout the play the screech of gulls and the wash of the tide below can be heard. Entrances to and from the harbour and ferry were made through the auditorium for the production at the King's Head, and the porch was downstage. This edition follows the conceit employed at the King's Head*

Robert Hanson, an old friend of the family, is heard off. He is in his sixties, proud and principled, yet never priggish. He enters, carrying a bottle of whisky

Robert (*calling*) Hallo! Stella! ... Anybody home ...?

Mrs Tucket, the Martyn's long-standing housekeeper from the village, also in her sixties, enters from the pantry door, L, *carrying her basket and outdoor shoes*

Good-evening.

Mrs Tucket Oh, evening, sir. Mrs Martyn's just gone up to the village, see if she can get any whisky from the *Ferry Inn*.

Robert Oh, I could have saved her the trouble! Just remembered I had this hidden away on my boat. (*He shows her the bottle and places it on top of the piano, on a drinks tray*)

Mrs Tucket (*changing out of her work shoes and overall into her civvies*) She will be pleased, sir. She had half a bottle of gin, but it seems that Mr Davies won't touch anything except whisky.

Robert Well, you have to take what you can get these days and be grateful.

Mrs Tucket Oh, you know what she is, sir. The children only have to ask for something and it's theirs. And she'll be just the same now with Mr Davies. We've been turning this place upside down all day to get it ready. Not that I mind hard work ——

Robert (*interrupting*) Yes, well I'm sure Mrs Martyn will be very glad of your help, and Miss Cherry too.

Mrs Tucket (*correcting him*) Ah!

Robert Oh, but we mustn't call her Miss Cherry anymore, must we?

Mrs Tucket Mrs Davies. It'll take a bit of getting used to.

Robert I suppose Mrs Martyn's very excited?

Mrs Tucket Over the moon! Talking 'bout grandchildren already, and how she wants to build on a new wing. Well, you've seen what she's done to the attic?

Robert No, what?

Mrs Tucket Turned it into a studio for Mr Davies. You wouldn't recognize it from what it was. Decorated the whole thing herself in two days. Have a look. (*She makes to open the studio door*)

Robert Er, no. I think I'll wait until he asks me.

Mrs Tucket (*picking up the local paper from a chair*) There's quite a bit about him in the newspaper. With his photograph and so on. Have you seen it?

Robert Yes, I saw it at the club.

Mrs Tucket Quite famous he seems to be. Pictures in galleries and so on. Have you seen any of them?

Robert Er, no, can't say that I have.

Mrs Tucket Mm, well, boats are more in your line, aren't they, sir? Well it's lovely for Miss Cherry to be married and it's lovely for her mother to have her home again. But I know Mrs Martyn would have liked it better if she'd come home sooner and had a proper wedding down here.

Robert Not much chance of a proper wedding with a girl like Cherry for a daughter and an artist for a son-in-law.

Mrs Tucket Suppose not. And then Miss Cherry was always one for having her own way.

Robert Spoilt! Always been the trouble. Same with the brother too, but perhaps the navy'll knock some of that out of him. Their mother's been too good to them all these years.

Mrs Tucket You're right there.

Robert checks his watch and moves downstage to look out of the window towards the harbour. A ferry horn is heard

Robert Well, I suppose they'll be here any minute now. The ferry's in, looks like them coming ashore now.

Mrs Tucket joins him at the window

Mrs Tucket Oh yes! That's them. Oh dear. Mrs Martyn will be so upset that she's not here to meet them.
Robert I should run up to the village if I were you. Warn her that the happy pair are about to descend on her.
Mrs Tucket I think I'd better. Oh, you'll stay, sir?
Robert Not on your life! No, I'll look in again later, when they've broken the ice. Besides, I've got my boat to put to bed. Evening.
Mrs Tucket Evening, sir.

Robert exits R

Mrs Tucket, in a panic now, grabs her basket from the chair, checks once more in the window and leaves, R

A moment's pause. Gulls and wash are heard

Cherry Davies is heard calling, off. She is lively, unpredictable, noncon-formist and in her early twenties. She enters from the harbour

Cherry Mother! Mother!

Evan Davies follows her in reluctantly. He is in his late twenties and is initially uneasy in his new surroundings. His stern manner conceals a quiet, brooding nature

They both carry their luggage, which they dispose of on the porch steps. Cherry crosses to the kitchen door and calls out as Evan enters the room. He stares about him and takes in the view

Mother! You here? ... Evan, she's not here. She can't have forgotten us. (*She sees some letters on top of the piano and picks them up*) Oh, letters. Mrs Davies ... Mrs Davies ... Mrs Davies! Why does something as simple as marriage make friends so ecstatic? I can't possibly answer them all, I wouldn't know what to say. (*She sees the whisky*) Oh, Evan, whisky! Wonderful. Just like Mother to remember. (*She senses his silence*) What's the matter?
Evan This room. You described it very badly.
Cherry Did I? Are you disappointed?
Evan God no! It's perfect. The sort of room I've always wanted.

Cherry I told you it was lovely. You never listen to a word I say. (*She moves towards the window*) I bet you thought it was going to be a dreadful seaside villa with a flag-pole in the garden! (*She moves next to him and stands looking out*) It's so good to be home again. (*She sees Robert and moves across to the porch to call out to him*) Robert! ... Robert! (*She moves back to Evan*) There goes Mother's faithful boyfriend, out with his boat. I can never tell which he loves more. That boat or Mother. (*She shouts again*) Robert! ... Come up and have a drink!

Evan Oh for Christ's sake, don't start throwing parties! It's all I can do to face my mother-in-law.

Cherry Robert's not a party. Anyway, you'll have to meet him sooner or later. He runs everything down here, from the hospital to the Boy Scouts. (*She reassures him*) And anyway, I've told you a thousand times that Mother's the easiest thing in the world. She's remembered your whisky anyhow. Surely that's one good mark in her favour. (*She moves away again*) Oh! You've no idea what it is for Jimmy and me to get down here and relax, knowing we don't have to do a damn thing because Mother'll do it all for us. Even down to mending our knickers!

Evan Well knowing the state of yours, I should think they keep her very busy.

Cherry Oh, ha, ha! I can't be bothered with that sort of thing. Never could and never will. But Mother's thoroughly domestic and old-fashioned. I always tell her she ought to have lived a hundred years ago.

Evan You fill me with more and more dread. I won't know what to say to her at all.

Cherry You don't have to say anything if you don't feel like it. Mother will rattle on quite happily. And, like all her generation, she has a mind like a sink. Enjoys nothing so much as a good dirty joke.

Evan My range of jokes is very limited. And any sense of humour I started out with is fast vanishing. If it wasn't for the charm of this room and the view of the harbour, I'd catch the first train back to London.

Cherry You wouldn't dare! (*She looks towards the studio door*) I wonder what she meant about a surprise in the attic?

She opens the door and climbs up the stairs, giving a surprised gasp when she sees the studio

Evan remains transfixed at the window

(*Off*) Oh! Evan!

Evan (*calmly*) What's the matter?

Cherry (*off*) Ha! It's unbelievable! She's turned the attic into a studio. Come and see!

Evan (*to himself*) I don't want a studio. (*He calls off to Cherry*) I want to look at this view.

Cherry (*off*) You've got the same view from here, only better. Come on!

Evan (*conceding*) Oh, all right. (*To himself, as he moves up*) What's the old lady done? Bought me a box of paints and an easel? (*He calls to her again*) I didn't come here to paint. I came to lie in the sun and fish.

Cherry appears back at the top of the steps

Cherry You can't lie in the sun in Cornwall. It rains every other day. And all the fish have defected to the East coast. (*She takes him by the arm and pulls him towards the steps*) Besides, you've got to work. I only married you because you were famous, and you can't disappoint me now! Come on!

Evan groans and climbs the stairs

Cherry remains below, waiting for his reaction. Evan whistles in surprise at what greets him

What did I tell you! What the hell is Mother doing? It's so unlike her not to be on the spot with open arms. I wonder if she's gone up to the village for anything?

Evan (*off*) Let her stay there then. The thought of meeting a mother-in-law reminds me of every music-hall joke I ever heard.

He re-enters and looks about him

What did I do with all my junk?

Cherry (*indicating where they entered*) Dumped it all on the porch. Do you want to see the rest of the house?

Evan Not particularly. I never want to move out of this room. Come and help me carry my stuff.

They move out to the porch and, ad lib, bring their luggage into the room. Evan places his paints on the piano stool, UC, and leans his easel against the open studio door. Cherry knocks his rucksack against the piano

Evan Watch that bag will you! There's a bottle of whisky in it!

Cherry Oh, Evan. Don't get plastered too early will you? I want you to make a good impression.

Evan I'll get plastered as soon as it suits me.

Cherry Well, in that case I'll leave you to it and go and warn Mother what to expect. She can't have gone far.

Cherry exits towards the harbour

Evan, still unpacking his luggage, calls after her

Evan Well, if she's dishing out soup at the Women's Institute, let her stay there. I can look after myself!

Evan collects a few things together and exits up to the studio

A brief pause

Stella Martyn enters from the door, R, in a hurry. She is in her late forties and has a natural, unforced personality and beauty. She carries roses and a whisky bottle. She looks around quickly and then goes to place the whisky on the piano. In doing so she sends Evan's paint box crashing to the ground, spilling its contents across the floor

Evan (*off; shouting from the studio*) For Christ's sake, don't touch my things!

Evan appears at the studio door, obviously surprised but not giving anything away

Stella remains frozen for a few moments, while she decides how to minimize the embarrassment

Stella (*eventually*) How do you do? I'm Mother.

She holds out her hand. He declines to shake it

Evan How do you do?
Stella Do I kiss you?
Evan I don't know.
Stella (*awkwardly*) It's absurd. I've no idea how to behave. I've never had a son-in-law before.
Evan (*simply*) Perhaps I'm the first of many.

She glances at him briefly, uncertain if it was a joke or not

Stella Where's Cherry?

Evan Gone to look for you.

Stella Oh, I went up to the village to get some whisky. Cherry said you drank a lot. Do you?

Evan 'Fraid so.

Stella Wish it wasn't so difficult to get. I'll have to go around bribing people ... I only drink myself when I have something rather terrible to face, like speaking to the Women's Institute or to the Bishop. (*Pause*) I rather feel like drinking something now ...

Evan Oh, am I as bad as that?

Stella Sorry, I didn't mean to be rude.

Evan Not rude at all. It's the most natural thing in the world to be apprehensive with the stranger who's descended out of the blue into your home.

Stella Oh, I'm not apprehensive, just curious. This has all been so exciting for me. You see, I live alone so much; I have the misfortune to be one of those mothers who are idiotic about their children.

Evan So I gather. (*He starts pouring a glass of whisky*)

Stella And it all happened so suddenly. I knew that Cherry *would* marry, but not for years. So, if I get hysterical and burst into tears, don't take any notice. But I am happy. Really happy.

Evan (*handing her the glass*) Are you? So am I.

Stella Of course, Cherry mentioned you from time to time, in her letters, but I'd no idea there was anything serious between you. You know, you're quite different from that photograph in the paper — that awful beard.

Evan Very old photograph. I haven't had a beard for years.

Stella Promise never to again.

Evan I don't make promises.

Stella Oh, I see. A difficult man!

Evan Very.

Stella And with your food.

Evan Extremely.

Stella Allergic to lobster?

Evan Can't touch it.

Stella Then you won't get any supper tonight.

A pause as Evan realizes he may have met his match

Evan Don't worry. Lobster is one of my favourite dishes.

Stella And globe artichokes?

Evan One of my passions. How could you know?

Stella Intuition. My one quality. I've no brains at all, as Cherry has probably told you.

Evan Cherry has told me nothing; or what she has told me was completely wrong.

Stella (*searching*) Why *did* you marry my precious daughter?

Evan She cleans my paintbrushes better than I do.

Stella How interesting. Is that all you demand in a wife?

Evan Not quite all. Cherry's good at answering the telephone and telling people I've left London, when I haven't. And she knows a good picture from a bad one.

Stella Oh, well surely that's very important.

Evan Very. Especially when we look at *other* people's pictures. Like all artists, I dislike being told the truth about my own.

Stella Of course, she thinks everything you do is wonderful.

Evan By no means. She's far too intelligent for that. But she grades my work as being about fifteen per cent better than anybody else's, which I find flattering. Even comforting. The war took quite a slice out of my painting life, so I've got to make up for all that now.

Stella Well, you seem to be succeeding — judging by the newspapers. And, er, what about Cherry? Has she any talent, do you think?

Evan You want me to be truthful?

Stella Please. I should hate a son-in-law to be anything else.

Evan She can turn out a fairly decent card ... spray of lilies in a vase. ... That's about it.

Stella I see. What a blessing she didn't go in for singing. Such an expensive training. The Art School was comparatively cheap; apart from the flat in Chelsea. However, if she's learnt to clean out your brushes then the family fortune hasn't been entirely wasted.

Evan On the contrary, it's been invested. And another thing I found out about Cherry quite early on was that she knew all the pubs in Chelsea where you can buy whisky by the bottle.

Stella Well, the Wrens are supposed to encourage initiative aren't they? She certainly didn't learn that at St Mary's.

Stella moves off to the pantry to collect a vase, talking all the while

(*Off*) Well, it's all very different from when I was young and newly married. Very exciting for both of you, but I can't help feeling that young people get married nowadays for ... well, strange reasons. Quite different from the reasons I got married for in nineteen twenty-seven.

Evan (*speaking in her direction*) Quite different. You see, the things you got married for then were still difficult to obtain *without* marriage. Nowadays they're handed to you on a plate.

Stella returns with a vase

Stella (*confused*) I don't think I know what you mean.
Evan I'm delighted to hear it!

Evan helps himself to some more whisky

Stella (*watching him*) Good thing we've got three bottles. Cherry and I will stick to lemonade.
Evan What happens when we run dry?
Stella We go across to the *Ferry Inn*, and you pay. (*She arranges the roses in the vase*) Tell me, d'you like your studio?
Evan I like everything. The studio, the harbour, the view — and this room above all. All your doing?
Stella Yes.
Evan Intuition again?
Stella I suppose so. Houses, food, looking after people has always been my job. Like painting is yours. I'm very ignorant you know. I know nothing about ——
Evan Nothing about what?
Stella Painting.
Evan You don't have to.
Stella I fell in love with an artist once, but he was unsuccessful, not like you.
Evan What happened to him?
Stella I don't know. I married a sailor instead.
Evan Very wise of you. What decided you?
Stella All that gold braid and knowing there'd be crossed swords at the wedding.
Evan (*humoured*) Ah! A shallow girl! No deep emotions.
Stella Not then. A uniform meant everything, even the policeman's on the corner. (*She changes the subject*) You are going to make Cherry happy, aren't you?
Evan Haven't thought about it.
Stella Then it's time you did.
Evan How do I start?
Stella By letting her know she's the most important thing in your life.
Evan But she isn't. My work's much more important.

A pause. Stella is taken aback at this news

Stella I think I'll have another drink!

Evan re-fills her glass

I'm serious, you know. Marriage is a very solemn business.

Evan Oh, it's not worth being solemn about anything these days.

Stella What's "these days" got to do with anything? That's just an excuse for careless behaviour. Thank heavens I had puritan parents who brought me up with a pre-nineteen-fourteen mentality. My marriage was happy for that reason.

Evan I wonder.

Stella What do you wonder?

Evan If that was the reason you were happy. I doubt if "pre-nineteen-fourteen mentality" had anything to do with it.

Stella Give me a better reason then?

Evan (*slyly*) Blessed are the pure in heart, for they shall see God!

Stella That's blasphemous!

Cherry calls from off R

Cherry (*off*) Mother!

Evan (*concluding*) Probably!

Cherry enters R

Stella (*seeing Cherry and placing her glass on the table*) Darling!

They embrace and hug each other tightly

Oh! I think I'm going to cry!

Cherry Don't be an idiot! What is there to cry about?

Stella Oh, everything! (*She glances over Cherry's shoulder and speaks to Evan*) See, I told you this would happen.

Cherry (*standing back*) You're so sentimental! Weddings, christenings, the National Anthem! Everything reduces you to a state of pulp. Look at you! I know all the signs, your hands are shaking and your hair's out of place.

Evan That's the whisky.

Cherry You've not been giving her whisky? Fatal!

Stella Cherry!

Cherry Well! I've been sweating up to the village to look for you and all the while, you've been sitting here getting sozzled with my husband. You ought to be ashamed of yourself! (*She hugs Evan*) Well, what do you think? Nicer than you expected?

Stella Much.

Evan Oh. What did you expect?

Stella That bearded man in the newspaper with long hair falling down his collar.

Evan Mm, speaking of which, I'm going to get out of this — which is choking me. I'll go and change.

Stella Oh, wonderful! (*To Cherry*) I do want him to look artistic for when Robert comes in. He'll be here in a minute.

Evan Who's Robert?

Cherry I told you. Mother's old boyfriend. He's been in love with her ever since Daddy died, and probably before that. He proposes to her regularly, once a month. It's routine. Like the new moon or the turn of the tide.

Stella Don't give me away!

Evan (*from the studio stairs*) I see. And is it also routine for you to refuse?

Stella Of course.

Evan Another Cornish Rhapsody!

He exits up the stairs

Stella (*calling after him*) Oh, if you want to change, Cherry will show you to your room.

Evan (*off*) This is my room!

Cherry crosses and closes the studio door shut

Cherry Damn!

Stella (*confused*) Mm?

Cherry I ought to have told you. We don't sleep together.

Stella Oh?

Cherry What I mean is, we don't share a room. Evan loathes it. He says it's the end of everything.

Stella Wasn't in my day ...

Cherry Your day was different.

Stella Must've been.

Cherry Besides, remember, Evan's an artist. Artists aren't like other men.

Stella Aren't they? What do you mean? Do tell me.

Cherry Oh, don't say "Do tell me" like that, as if there was something weird about Evan! Honestly, Mother. Your generation is obsessed with sex, you think of nothing else!

Stella We're not, and I don't!

Cherry Look, all you have to do is put the sheets and things on that divan in the studio. He's crazy about the room already.

Stella That means he'll have to come trailing down here in the dark, across the hall and up the stairs if he wants to go to your room.

Cherry Well? What of it?

Stella Daddy would never have done it for me.

Cherry Well if Evan wants to go paddling around in the dark that's his funeral.

Stella I think it very probably will be.

Cherry You've had too much whisky, darling. You know how one drink flies to your head.

Stella It doesn't! I've got a very strong head. Much stronger than yours if you want to be personal. And I was perfectly sober when I got engaged to be married, and I'm beginning to think that you weren't.

Cherry I know, darling. You were on a yacht at Cowes ... there was a full moon ... someone played the Eton boating song ... and Daddy said, "Why can't this go on forever". Quite different from Evan and me. It was pouring with rain in the King's Road and we were both tight.

Stella How terribly unromantic.

Cherry No. It was great fun. Evan performed reams of *Hamlet*, and nearly fell in the gutter. That was when his door key fell down the drain, so he had to come back and spend the night with me.

Stella I don't believe a word of it! You've always exaggerated since the age of three, when you pretended that Nanny hit you with an iron!

Cherry (*protesting*) She used to strap Jimmy and me to our beds with electric wires.

Stella Rubbish! She was a strict Nonconformist and adored you.

They share the joke

Cherry Anyway, Evan and I did get engaged walking down the King's Road in an ... alcoholic haze. Neither of us can remember whether it was that night or the following morning we decided to become engaged.

Stella That night I should hope! Darling, if I'd known this was the way you were behaving in Chelsea, I'd never have allowed you to take that flat.

Cherry Why on earth not? It was all perfectly harmless. (*Innocently*) If you love a person who gets tiddly, the least you can do is take him home and give him your bed.

Stella (*concealing her surprise*) Well, all I can say is that I'm extremely relieved that everything has worked out as it has done.

Cherry Saves a lot of trouble doesn't it?

Stella Mm?

Cherry Getting married, I mean. Amazing how stupid some hotels still are about things like that.

Stella (*realizing*) Cherry. You ... you don't mean that you went away together before you were married?

Cherry Of course. God, darling! I've known Evan ages. Nearly six months. What did you expect us to do at weekends? Go to Kew?

Stella I don't pretend to know what goes on nowadays. It's utterly beyond me. If I'd done such a thing when I was your age, well ... I don't know what would have happened.

Cherry I do. A nervous breakdown, or a baby! Probably both. Besides during those few days Evan and I spent in Cumberland, we went for long walks and discussed Van Gogh.

Stella And what about the evenings?

Cherry Played Gin Rummy and slept like logs.

Stella Well, I can't think why you bothered to go all the way to Cumberland for that.

Cherry snarls, impatient at being questioned

All right, all right, don't make that face at me! If your behaviour was unorthodox before you were married, it's even more so now. Come along to the linen cupboard and get the sheets. Mrs Tucket will be frightfully shocked in the morning!

Stella moves to the kitchen door, L

Cherry Why?

Stella (*in her best Mrs Tucket impression*) "Married only a fortnight and separate rooms". Course she'll be shocked!

Cherry (*following Stella out*) Disgusting old woman!

They leave

A moment's pause. A ferry hoots

Evan enters from the studio. He crosses to the drinks tray on the piano and takes a bottle of whisky, then moves back to the stairs. He stops. He turns back and takes another bottle of whisky, then exits off. Having deposited the bottles in his room, he returns and proceeds to pour himself a large whisky. After a moment there is a tentative knocking on the door, R. *A second later Robert peers in and, for the first time, sees Evan*

Robert (*cautiously*) Oh, er, good-evening. You're, er, Cherry's husband I take it?

Evan I am. (*Pause*) Come in. Have a drink.

Robert steps into the room, still unsure

Robert Well, er, seeing it's my whisky you're making so free with, I think I will.

Evan Oh, well that's very kind of you. Are you the landlord of the *Ferry Inn*?

Robert (*eyeing him*) No. I'm Robert Hanson and I'm an old friend of your mother-in-law's.

Evan Oh yes, of course. Robert! (*He winks at Robert, knowingly*)

Robert (*baffled*) Sorry?

Evan The new moon, the turn of the tide! Here, have some of your whisky. It'll give you courage for the next time!

He hands Robert a glass of whisky. Robert is now more uneasy than ever

Have you come to supper?

Robert No, merely to offer my congratulations.

Evan What for?

Robert Your marriage of course.

Evan Oh, bit early for that, isn't it? I'd keep them for at least six months, if I were you. I mean, the whole thing about marriage is a bit of a toss up isn't it? D'you know the story about the man who married the opera singer? He took one look at her after the wedding night and said, "For God's sake sing!" I always feel that's what most people must feel like.

Robert Mm. You, er, you met Cherry at some party in London, I believe?

Evan I don't remember a party ... never go to them. No, Cherry wandered into one of my favourite bars in Chelsea and I bought her a drink.

Robert When I was young, that sort of thing used to happen in Leicester Square.

Evan Probably still does. We're more respectable in Chelsea. It's the girls who propose.

Robert Yes, well I'm afraid that sort of talk is beyond me. The war doesn't seem to have improved manners or morals. Pity I think.

Evan Manners are lousy, I grant you, but morals are pretty much what they always were. To the pure, all things are impure. But don't run away with the idea that Cherry led a "loose life" in London. As far as I know she was amazingly unattached for someone of her age.

Robert So I should hope.

Evan You ought to see *some* of them, Robert. They should be kept in cages. More whisky?

Robert (*covering his glass*) Er, no. No, thank you. I must say, I didn't think much of the friends that Cherry brought down here before. Perhaps you'll put a stop to all that?

Evan I wouldn't dream of putting a stop to anything. Cherry's private life is her own affair. How long have you known the family?

Robert Getting on for fifteen years. They came to live down here when Stella's husband retired from the Navy. And then of course, he died shortly after. Yes, I taught your Cherry how to sail. She always was a tomboy, even then.

Evan Still is, by nature. Happy anywhere. Stick her in Holloway Gaol and she'd settle down. Makes it all very easy for me.

Robert, completely thrown by Evan's indifference, crosses L to place his empty glass on the table; he takes in the sinking level of the whisky bottle as he does so

Robert You, er ... you going to be down here for long?

Evan For life, I imagine. I've never seen a place I like better.

Robert Well, I'd better warn you. Houses are extremely hard to come by in these parts.

Evan (*confused*) What's wrong with this one?

Robert This one happens to belong to your mother-in-law.

Evan Oh, that's all right. We can all live here together. An "enchanting prospect".

Robert Mm, well perhaps she wouldn't think so. And anyway, a young couple ought to have a place to themselves.

Evan I disagree. And any place run by Cherry would be a pigsty in five minutes. You should've seen her place in London. I spent the night there once. Never again!

Stella and Cherry enter from the door, L, carrying between them blankets, sheets and pillows

Stella Oh, hallo, Bob. Just in time for a drink. (*She glances at the two men*) You've introduced yourselves?

Robert (*meaningfully*) Oh yes.

Stella moves R, to Evan, whilst Robert embraces Cherry for the first time. They ad lib hallos, etc.

Evan (*to Stella*) It's his whisky we've been drinking.

Robert (*to Cherry*) Hallo, my dear. Congratulations!

Stella (*to Evan*) What happened to the other two bottles?

Robert and Cherry turn in to listen

Evan (*innocently*) Upstairs, by my bed.

Robert vocalizes something disapproving. Stella immediately defuses the situation by jumping in to play hostess

Stella Bob, you must take Evan out sailing. Cherry tells me he's crazy to fish. Isn't that so, Evan?
Evan Correct. (*Directly to Robert, mockingly*) I intend to fish every day, wet or fine, Bob.
Stella (*defusing again*) The scenery is wonderful all around this coast. Some people prefer the North, but I always think it's far too bare and windswept. Here we have so many little bays and lovely valleys and wild flowers and gulls wheeling about the harbour. Perfect for painting.
Cherry (*to quieten her*) Yes, but Mother, darling, Evan doesn't paint landscapes.
Stella Oh. Doesn't he? What *do* you paint, Evan?
Evan The female figure in undress.

Robert, draining the dregs of his glass, chokes

Stella (*nonplussed*) Ah, yes. Nudes. Of course. Wonderful in a gallery, but out of place in a room like this, I always think.
Evan I agree. (*With a look to Robert*) There's nothing so unattractive as the average naked woman. (*He smiles. To Stella*) What are you doing with those sheets?
Stella Taking them to your studio. Not intuition this time. Cherry's orders.
Evan Sorry. D'you mind?
Stella Mind? Why should I mind? It's not my honeymoon.

Robert, realizing he is totally out of his depth, moves across R to the door

Robert Yes, well, I must be getting along.
Stella Oh, must you? Oh, don't go yet. (*She hands Evan her share of the bed linen*) Evan, would you mind making up your own bed?
Evan (*taking it*) I always have done.

Evan exits into the studio

Robert waits by the door, only staying for Stella's sake. Cherry moves to the studio stairs

Cherry I'll give you a hand. Night Robert.

Robert Good-night, Cherry.
Stella Oh, darling, the roses.

Stella picks up the vase of roses from the table and hands them to Cherry on the stairs. Cherry gives her mother a knowing wink and a nudge, in Robert's direction. Stella glares and playfully pats Cherry's behind

Cherry disappears up the stairs, closing the door after her

An awkward pause

Stella (*hopefully*) He's, er, charming. Don't you think?
Robert Yes, well. I prefer to reserve my opinion.
Stella Oh, I know that voice. That means you dislike him.
Robert Well, he's had a jolly good swig at my whisky.
Stella Was that your whisky, Bob? How sweet of you.
Robert Well, I promised you, didn't I?
Stella Yes, but I know how difficult it is to get. You shouldn't have bothered.
Robert (*taking her hands*) Now, Stella, I want you to promise me something in return; now don't you go running around after these two. Let them take care of themselves. They're perfectly capable of it.
Stella But I love doing it.
Robert Maybe. But I know that artistic type. He'll dig himself in here, probably drink you out of house and home, and you'll be the one to suffer from it.

Stella moves away to collect the stray glasses that have accumulated in the room

Stella I think you're being very unfair to Evan, Bob. You can't possibly judge him after two minutes. Besides, this is only a holiday! Cherry told me he'd had some wonderful offer from New York, just the other day. They're bound to do a lot of travelling.
Robert Well he told me just now he intends to settle here for life.

Stella has reached the piano and stops, visibly pleased at the news

Stella Oh, oh did he? I couldn't be more pleased. (*She moves off again*) I must go and change and see about some supper. Are you sure you won't stay? It's hot lobster, you know, and plenty of it.
Robert (*checking his watch*) No, no thanks. There's a meeting of the Harbour Board and I'm late already.

Stella (*heading for the door,* L) Oh well.
Robert (*stalling her*) Er, Stella.
Stella (*turning back, aware of what's coming*) Yes ... ?
Robert (*uneasily*) If, er ... if they do, er ... if they do decide to, er, stay here
and make it their home, there's ... there's a house at the top of the hill that's
been crying out for you to take charge of it for a very long while now.
Stella Dear Bob.
Robert All right, all right. I won't bore with the old story now. But, you know
what I mean, don't you?
Stella I do. Bless you.

*Robert, mission accomplished, tentatively pecks her on the cheek and moves
back to the door,* R

Robert Well, good-night, my dear.
Stella Good-night, Bob.

Robert exits

*Stella stands looking to the door for a moment then shakes herself back into
action*

Cherry appears at the studio door

Cherry Has he gone?
Stella Yes.
Cherry Evan wants to know if it was "the old routine"?
Stella (*at the door,* L) Tell Evan to mind his own business!

Stella exits, taking the whisky glasses with her

*Cherry moves into the room and looks out downstage, to the harbour. A ferry
hoots. She moves up to the piano and plays a few notes, improvising*

*After a few moments, Evan appears at the bottom of the stairs. They smile
at each other*

Evan (*looking around*) Where's she gone?
Cherry (*from the piano stool*) Oh, to mix the salad and look at the lobster,
I suppose. And to drape herself in what she calls her "tea-gown". She's very
old-fashioned, you know. The war didn't alter her at all. And she is thrilled
by your arrival. Wait till you see the supper she's prepared, and it's all for

your benefit. When she's alone she has bread and butter and a cup of tea.

Evan sits beside her on the piano stool and strums a few chords

Evan (*mimicking*) "Cup of tea"!
Cherry Yes! Apt, don't you think?

She gets up and stands behind him

Go on, try it out. It's probably very tinny. No-one ever plays it.

Evan plays the first few bars of "Little Boy Blues", by Vivian Ellis

Cherry (*laughing*) What on earth is that? I've never heard it before!
Evan Not your vintage. Pre-war.
Cherry News to me you can play this stuff. I thought you hated it?
Evan (*still playing*) Did you? But then you know very little about me, one way and another.
Cherry Think so?

Stella enters from the door, L, now dressed in her favourite "tea-gown". She carries three dinner-napkins and rings

Stella Oh! My favourite song! How did you know?
Evan Intuition.
Stella (*dancing to the music, quite carried away*) How it takes me back!
Cherry Now she'll be well away. Darling, you are so incredibly sentimental!
Stella I'm not sentimental. I'm romantic. There's all the difference in the world, isn't there, Evan?
Evan Between sentiment and romance? No difference at all. I wallow in both.
Cherry You liar! You're the cynic of all time!
Evan So you think. But I'm Jekyll and Hyde. (*In a* Hammer Horror *voice*) "You only know Hyde". .

Evan changes the tune to "Vilja", from The Merry Widow, *by Lehàr. Stella swoons and then waltzes to it*

Cherry You'll have Mother in tears in a minute; then we won't get any supper at all. (*She dances in to Stella*) You look very sweet and you smell heavenly, darling. But then you always do. (*She backs off to the door,* R) I'll wash my hands, but I needn't change need I?

Cherry stops at the door to collect her suitcase and bags

Stella Of course not, if you don't want to.

Cherry opens the door

Evan (*to Cherry*) Slut!

Cherry pauses for a brief second in the doorway, before deciding to ignore him and continue out

Stella (*bemused*) Is that the usual way for a bridegroom to address his bride?
Evan It is when you've a bride like Cherry. (*He stops playing to turn and look at Stella*) That's a lovely dress you're wearing.
Stella (*modestly*) Oh, it's years old and faded. But I always change, even when I'm alone.

Stella is now engrossed in rolling the dinner-napkins into their rings at the table

Evan You're very paintable.
Stella (*smartly*) Thought you only painted nudes?
Evan Only when I lack other inspiration.
Stella Oh, don't stop. Play that first one again!

Evan picks up the original tune. Stella moves in to lean on the left of the piano

Yes, that's it.

They both sing a few lines, helping each other to remember as they do so

Yes. *Baby June* wasn't it?
Evan } (*together*) *Clowns in Clover*!
Stella }

They sing some more

Stella My mother took me to see it, on my birthday. I wore a bright pink frock and sobbed all through the last act! Is your mother alive?
Evan (*immediately*) No. She died of pneumonia when I was just fourteen.
Stella Poor boy.

Evan (*scoffing*) Huh! Unpleasant little bastard!

During the following, Evan finishes playing; he sits strumming a few chords while he listens to Stella

Stella We hurt so much when we're young, but then as you grow older, the pain seems to flatten out. No more crying into pillows ... no more stabs below the heart. All the same, when Jimmy went away to school, I wore dark glasses for a week! If anyone spoke to me, I burst into tears. Then he returned ... changed beyond recognition.

Evan He'll come back again one day, you know. They always do, like homing pigeons.

A dinner-gong is heard offstage

Stella (*bringing herself back to reality*) Supper! Cherry's hungry.

As Stella makes to move to the door, L, Evan strikes up playing

Evan To hell with supper!

He runs his fingers down the keys and starts again with "Little Boy Blues". They both sing once more

After a moment, Cherry enters, wondering where they have got to. She sees them exactly where she left them. She tries to extract her mother to the kitchen, but fails, so she moves back towards the door, R

Cherry (*over their singing*) Well for God's sake!

Cherry exits

Stella and Evan complete the song, with Stella back at the piano. They laugh and share their accomplishment, looking at each other properly — for the first time

Stella exits L, taking the dinner-napkins with her

The following business constitutes a cross-over to SCENE 2. Piano music—Satie— plays throughout and the action is continuous

Evan stands, closes the piano lid and begins to assemble his pallet and various brushes on to the piano. He changes into his apron

Mrs Tucket enters, R, with the easel, which she sets in position, UC. She pulls the piano stool DR and seats herself

SCENE 2

Two months later. Late afternoon

The Lights cross-fade to reveal Evan standing at his easel, UC. He is painting Mrs Tucket who is still seated on the piano stool, DR

The light is fading and there are long shadows

Evan And after your husband's *eleventh* operation, what did he do then?
Mrs Tucket Oh, he ... he rallied ... for a few months. But he was never what you could call "fit for hard work". No ... not once they removed the stone. As large as a pigeon's egg it was. ... Surgeon said he'd never seen anything like it ... no wonder my poor Tom had gone off his food. (*She moves from her posed position*)
Evan (*concentrating on his portrait, half aloud*) No wonder at all.

Evan moves down to Mrs Tucket. She continues to talk, oblivious

Mrs Tucket But it was the bath up at the Infirmary that finished him off ... Sister should have known better. The shock. All that water and him not used to it. He said to the nurse as she led him up to it, "I shall die if you put me in there!" (*Pause*) And he did. (*She re-adjusts her pose*) A lovely husband he made me, Mr Davies. A lovely husband. Never an angry word and we were sweethearts right up till the end. ... (*With meaning*) That's what marriage ought to be about ... as I was saying to Mrs Martyn, only this morning. Whilst we were making up the beds.

She gives him a quick glance, to note any reaction. There is none, so she turns back

Keep courting, I said. That's the secret of a happy marriage. From the time you go up the aisle till the time you're carried down it at your funeral, keep courting.
Evan (*without looking up*) You must have led a very exhausting life, one way and another.
Mrs Tucket (*amused*) Get along with you! I'm sixty-five, but I don't feel

a day over twenty-five. I dare say I'm as young in heart as your Miss
Cherry. (*Significantly*) And twice as active.

Evan That wouldn't be difficult.

Mrs Tucket (*daring to go further*) I'll tell you one thing though, Mr Davies.
Though she is your wife, and a fine looking young woman; she'll never be
as good looking as her mother. (*She smiles as she recalls*) I've known Mrs
Martyn for, ooh ... nigh on twelve years now. And she's prettier now than
she's ever been. It's having you two down here to live that's done it. (*She
is now on a roll*) Well, stands to reason doesn't it? 'T'aint natural for a
woman to live alone. 'Specially a woman like Mrs Martyn.

Evan (*now intrigued*) Why not?

Mrs Tucket Because she's the giving kind. An' they're the sort who love
the longest.

*She re-positions herself, waiting for Evan to continue, but something has
struck him and he now stops*

Evan (*wiping a brush*) Well, I think that'll be all for today.

Mrs Tucket (*surprised*) Oh? You're finished with me?

Evan Yes.

Mrs Tucket (*implying "Was it something I said"*) Oh? Well, I ——

Evan Yes, we've had the best of the light.

*Mrs Tucket, relieved, straightens herself up and stands, rubbing a crick in her
neck. Evan cleans some brushes on a rag*

Mrs Tucket (*cautiously*) Can I ... can I see?

Evan Sure. Go ahead.

*Evan stands aside as Mrs Tucket nervously approaches. She stares at the
portrait for a few moments, obviously flattered and pleased*

Mrs Tucket Ooh! (*She is for once speechless*)

Evan Like it?

Mrs Tucket Ooh! It's what you'd call a ... "a speaking likeness".

Evan Glad you think so.

*Mrs Tucket, now happily flustered, moves off out of the door, L, to collect
her basket and cardigan, ad libbing as she goes: "Well, I had no idea it was
going to look like that, my word", etc.*

Mrs Tucket (*off, a sudden thought*) 'Ere, Mr Davies.

She comes back in

Will, er, will this be hung up in a gallery in London?

Evan I dare say.

Mrs Tucket (*doubly flustered*) Oh! What, with strangers coming in to look at it?

Evan Hundreds.

Cherry is heard calling from the harbour

Cherry (*off*) Evan!

Evan (*continuing*) Probably have to have policemen to keep the crowds back.

Mrs Tucket (*believing every word*) Did you ever!

Cherry enters, from the harbour, in sailing gear and lifebelt

Cherry (*breathlessly*) Lost by half a minute! I only hope everyone heard our language! (*She takes off her lifebelt and dumps it* DR) Well? How's it going?

Evan Fine. Just packing up.

Mrs Tucket (*standing guard at the easel*) Oh, Miss Cherry. Come and look at my portrait.

Cherry does so

Proper stylish, innit?

Cherry (*truly impressed*) Bloody good!

Evan moves around the easel to stand beside Cherry as Mrs Tucket pulls on her cardigan

Evan Mm, not bad. I'll have to do something about the left eye. It's all over the shop.

Mrs Tucket (*indignantly*) What's wrong with my left eye?

Cherry Oh, don't worry. I'll see he doesn't spoil your beauty for you.

Mrs Tucket He'd better not! If he did there's plenty as'd want to know the reason why. (*She moves* R) Old Joe down at the ferry has been courting me steady for five years now.

Evan (*playfully*) Oh, Mrs T! I thought I was your only admirer?

Mrs Tucket Oh, get along with you! (*To Cherry*) Is there any more I can do for your mother, miss?

Cherry No, I shouldn't think so. She washed up after lunch and cleared up my room; so, I'd get along home for tea if I were you.

Mrs Tucket (*satisfied*) See you in the morning then. (*She puts her hand on the door latch*) And I'll be free for you at two o' clock, Mr Davies. If that's all right by Mrs Martyn. 'Tis a real pleasure to do it, you're welcome any time. Good-afternoon.

She exits

Cherry (*after a pause*) Garrulous old bitch!

Evan Why didn't she tell me that coming up here let her off work?

Cherry Only too glad to get away I expect.

Evan Has this been going on all the time she's been sitting for me?

Cherry Has what been going on?

Evan (*firmly*) Stella washing up and doing the things that Mrs Tucket usually does.

Cherry Of course. What of it? Mother doesn't mind.

Evan And d'you ever offer to help?

Cherry God no! I'd be terribly in the way.

Cherry looks through some of Evan's paintings

Evan Well you could at least tidy out your own room!

Cherry (*defensively*) Look, I made my bed! Anyway, I didn't get up until half-past twelve, and I've been sailing all afternoon.

Evan (*glancing towards the right door*) What do you suppose she's doing now?

Cherry Oh, washing out all the hair brushes, I imagine. I saw rows and rows of them laid out on her balcony just now. (*She discovers a portrait that takes her completely by surprise*) Oh, Evan! This is wonderful. When did you do it?

Evan (*suspiciously*) What have you got there?

Cherry This head of Mother.

Evan Put it down!

Cherry Why? What for? What's the matter?

Evan Give it to me!

Cherry (*equal to him*) God, you're funny!

A terrible silence as they both stare at each other, uncertainly

(*Apologetically*) Oh, I know. You were going to — do it as a surprise for my birthday. Was that it?

Evan (*after a pause, softly*) Yes.

Cherry Now I've spoilt all the fun. Sorry. I promise I won't look at it again. What a lovely idea. (*She replaces the portrait*) When have you been working on it? Mother hasn't said a word ——

Evan She doesn't know.

Cherry Doesn't know? What do you mean?

Evan She hasn't sat for it, I've been doing it from memory. ... Working early in the mornings.

Cherry How wonderful. Now I know why you asked for that alarm clock up there. Well, I never thought anything would get you up with the sun. But if that turns out to be the picture of all time, it'll be worth it! Exciting for Mother too, she'll get the thrill of her life.

Evan (*sharply*) Oh, for God's sake!

Cherry Don't be so scratchy. You know how delighted she'll be.

A pause. Evan, distressed that his work has been discovered, isolates himself and cleans his pallet. Cherry stands and moves in, R

Cherry Well, I must go and change if I'm going to the pictures with Pam. Are you coming?

Evan (*definitely*) No.

Cherry (*trying to coax him*) It's Ingrid Bergman. You know you like her.

Stella enters R *carrying a heavy basket of logs for the stove*

Evan No, I don't! She bores me stiff.

Stella Who bores you stiff?

Evan (*turning to take the basket from her*) What are you doing? I've told you about this before.

Evan takes the basket and places it next to the stove. Stella moves into the room and sees Evan's easel

Stella What are you arguing about?

Cherry I'm going to the pictures with Pam and I'm trying to persuade Evan to come with me.

Stella Oh, yes. Go with them, Evan.

Evan I don't want to.

Stella But you'd enjoy it.

Evan (*firmly*) No, I wouldn't.

Cherry realizes it is hopeless and moves to the door, R

Cherry Never force a man to do something he doesn't want to. I've learnt that much from marriage, if nothing else. Did you mend my trousers, darling?

Stella (*now at the easel*) Yes, they're on your bed.

Cherry (*pleadingly*) And can I borrow your new scarf?

Stella Course.

Cherry Thanks. I won't want any supper. We'll probably go on a pub crawl after the film and end up at the *White Hart.* (*She gives them a final look*) Well, take care of yourselves. (*To Stella*) Pamper him.

Cherry exits R

A silence. Evan is still preoccupied with the portrait. Stella watches him and takes in Mrs Tucket's picture

Stella (*eventually*) You should have gone with her.

Evan (*softly*) Why?

Stella It would have made her happy.

Evan moves to the piano stool and sits, looking downstage towards the harbour. Stella stands

Evan I've told you before, I'm not the sort of person to make others happy. Never have and never will be.

Stella Sometimes I get worried for you and Cherry.

Evan Why?

Stella Oh, I don't know. You're both so casual. I suppose I'm old-fashioned, but it's all so different from when I was young and newly married.

Evan It is different.

Stella moves to sit on the arm of the armchair, DL

Stella Having you here's not at all like I imagined. You don't do things together. Cherry goes off sailing on her own, or to the cinema like tonight; and you stay here all day and paint or play the piano and talk to me. I wonder if all modern marriages are so lacking in ...

Evan Lacking in what?

Stella Well, romance. To put it bluntly.

Evan Ah. You're thinking of your "gold braided past".

Stella No, not exactly. I don't know what I'm thinking of. Perhaps what I'd feel if I were Cherry.

Evan What would you feel?

Stella (*obviously having thought it out prior to this*) I'd want to spend every second with my husband, I'd want to be with him all the time ... Whether it was in a boat, or a studio, or anywhere. Just as long as we were together. I wouldn't have a mind of my own at all, really. (*She stands, a different intention*) Perhaps the war has killed that sort of instinct. I don't pretend to know what goes on in Cherry's mind. (*She looks at the bottles on top of the piano*) You're being very good with the whisky. What's happened to you?

Evan Haven't felt like whisky.

Stella Oh, would you rather something else?

Evan No, I don't want anything.

Stella It's that swim before breakfast that's done it. I time myself by you every morning. When I hear you dive off the harbour, I say to myself, "There's Evan. Half-past eight, time to get up".

Evan Do you?

Cherry calls, off R

Cherry (*off*) Bye then! I'm off.

Stella rushes across to the door to answer her

Stella Bye! Have a good time!

The front door is heard slamming. A pause. Stella closes the door and turns to Evan

I still think you should have gone with her.

Evan does not reply. Stella leans on the piano lid and perches there for a second. During the following, Evan studies Stella hard

I'm so glad you like this room, and that you're happy here. I wasn't sure if you would or not. I thought you might be temperamental and want to paint in the kitchen or something. (*She moves downstage*) I used to sit here by myself sometimes, when the children went to school. There was a funny old table there — (*she points* DC), and I'd mend the linen here on wet afternoons. I'd sit — for hours, listening to the water coming up on the slip below, and dreaming ... dreaming about nothing at all, really. It was still and peaceful.

Evan Don't move!

Stella What ... ?

Evan Please! Keep just as you were.

Evan is struck suddenly by a detail. For a moment we, like Stella, are unsure what is happening. Evan moves upstage and repositions his easel close to Stella, then picks up her portrait and sets it ready to work on. Stella does not see her portrait

Stella (*uneasily*) What's the matter?
Evan (*concentrating*) I was right ... that line at the corner of the mouth.
Stella What are you talking about?
Evan Be quiet!

A silence comes over them as Evan works with immense concentration on the portrait and Stella remains posed, rather awkwardly

Stella (*eventually*) How long do I have to remain like this?
Evan (*without looking up*) For as long as I tell you.

Pause

Stella (*seizing the idea*) Am I standing in for Mrs Tucket?
Evan (*half amused*) No, darling.

Stella takes a second to absorb his use of the word "darling". Evan works. There is a slight pause

Stella Evan, I've been wanting to talk to you about quite a lot of things ...
Evan What sort of things?
Stella Well, the future ... yours and Cherry's plans. What you're going to do ...
Evan I never make plans.
Stella Cherry told me that you'd had an offer from America only last week. Will you go?
Evan God no!
Stella Why not?
Evan Why should I go to America, when I'm happy here?
Stella Cherry might like it. You might like it. It might be good for you both.
Evan Do you want to get rid of us?
Stella Oh, no. No.
Evan Stop talking then and don't move your head!

Evan adds a couple more strokes to the picture, then stands back, satisfied

There. Finished. If I never paint another picture for the rest of my life, it won't matter. I've done what I wanted to do. I've done something good.
Stella (*still unaware of what it is*) May I look?
Evan If you want to.

Evan moves away from the easel, exposing his work, as Stella approaches. She stands looking at the portrait for a very long time. Quite still and almost with a blank expression, as her eyes well up. She stares until she can stand it no more and moves swiftly to the door, R

Evan (*knowing he has upset her*) Where are you going?
Stella (*leaving*) To my room!
Evan Why?
Stella Because I don't want you to see me cry!

Robert is heard, abruptly cutting in, from off R

Robert (*off*) Stella! Stella!

Stella quickly decides to come back into the room, rather than face Robert outside. She closes the door. Evan removes Stella's portrait from the easel and replaces it with Mrs Tucket's, just as Robert enters

Stella (*in reply*) I'm here!

Robert enters, R. He is dressed in his old work clothes, as if having come from his boat, and is quite wet from the rain

Robert Oh, it was so quiet, I thought everybody must be out.
Stella Evan was just showing me Mrs Tucket's portrait. It's very good.
Robert Oh? (*To Evan*) Am I permitted to look?
Evan Of course.

Robert moves across to look at the picture, from upstage of the easel. Evan stands aside

Robert (*obviously impressed but desperate to conceal it*) Mm. Yes, well. ... Well, you'd know it was Mrs Tucket all right.
Stella That's what I call a masterpiece of understatement! He means he likes it.
Evan (*indifferent*) I'm glad.
Robert Going to show it in New York, I suppose?

Evan What makes you think that?

Robert Oh, sort of thing that would appeal to them, isn't it? Local colour and all that. (*To Stella*) Besides, think of all the dollars it'd bring in.

Stella But Evan isn't going to New York, Bob.

Robert No? I gathered from Cherry there'd been some sort of offer? Perhaps I got hold of the wrong end of the stick. Where is she by the way?

Stella Gone to the pictures.

Robert (*with a glance to Evan*) All by herself?

Stella No, with Pam.

Robert Well it's going to be a filthy evening. She'll get very wet.

Stella Oh, she's got an oilskin.

Concerned at Stella's lack of interest, Robert moves downstage and gestures towards the harbour

Robert Yes, but it'll get stronger when the tide turns. There must've been a gale warning. They've hoisted the cone. You never know what will happen with this September tide. I've known more damage done at this time of year than in all the winter months put together. I remember once ——

Stella Have a drink, Bob?

Robert What? Er, no, I don't think so. I got pretty wet outside. I'm going straight home to change. As a matter of fact, Stella, I really came in to ask if you'd like to come up and have dinner with me tonight?

Stella I'm afraid I can't, Bob. You see, Cherry will come straight home after the film and want supper, and you know Mrs Tucket doesn't come back on Fridays. Another time, I'd love to.

Robert (*hurt*) Oh, well ...

Stella Anyway, if it's going to be as wet as you say ...

A loud rumble of thunder and a flash of lightning come just in time to help Stella out

Yes, here it comes. You'd better get home before you get soaked through.

Robert (*with a hint of sarcasm*) I have an oilskin too, you know? (*To Evan*) Don't forget to put that other anchor down. That is, if you know how.

Evan (*equally sarcastic*) I think I do.

Robert, realizing there is no more he can do, looks at them both for a brief second then, thinking he has caused an atmosphere himself, makes for the door, R

Robert Well, then. Er, don't bother to come down, Stella. I can see myself
out

He leaves

There is an awkward moment between Evan and Stella. Stella breaks it by moving DR *to pick up Cherry's lifebelt*

Evan He was right about the gale.
Stella Yes ...
Evan It's going to be bad.

Stella moves L, *with the lifebelt. Evan moves back up to the easel and removes Mrs Tucket's portrait*

(*Stopping Stella*) Why did you lie to him?
Stella Lie to him?
Evan Yes. First you said I was showing you Mrs Tucket's picture, then you said you couldn't have dinner with him because of Cherry. And you know Cherry's going to the *White Hart*.
Stella (*simply*) I'd forgotten.
Evan Had you?
Stella (*as before*) No.

She leaves by the door, L, *leaving Evan to ponder her intention. Reaching no certain conclusion he exits up the studio stairs, taking his painting apron and paint box with him. Stella returns, and moves downstage to the window. She watches the storm increasing*

Stella (*shouting up*) What are you going to do?
Evan (*off*) Put that anchor down, while I can still see it!
Stella Be careful, you're not very expert, remember? (*She is amused by the thought*)

Unseen by Stella, Evan re-enters carrying a pair of wellingtons and a waterproof overcoat

(*Calling behind her*) What do you want for supper?

Evan creeps up close behind her and bellows in an equal manner, causing Stella to jump

Evan *Omelette à la Esperanza!* (*He laughs at her surprise*) Learnt how to make them in Tenerife. Have you got any wine?

Stella Yes, one bottle of Nuits St Georges.

Evan Mm. We'll have that. You light the fire and bring in the wine. And that yellow dress, you haven't worn it lately?

Stella Oh, it's so old. All my clothes are. D'you know, I had that made in case James and I were ever asked to Buckingham Palace. We never were.

Evan Did you mind?

Stella Yes!

Evan Well wear it tonight.

Stella Don't be ridiculous! Are we celebrating something?

Evan Course. (*He starts to pull on his boots*) The first time that you and I have ever had dinner alone together!

He pulls the hood of his coat over his head, covering his eyes and making himself look playfully stupid. They both laugh

He moves across to the porch and disappears to the harbour

As he goes, a deafening crack of thunder accompanied by a flash of lightning cause Stella to dash back to the porch, looking worried

Stella (*loudly after him*) Evan! Be careful!

The following business is underscored with an intricate and essential sound score of thunder, wind and rain. The sound score continues under the dialogue and is used to heighten tension and specific lines

Satisfied that he has heard her, Stella returns inside. She moves DL *to the stove and proceeds to light the fire, adding a couple of logs. She then moves off through the door,* L, *into the kitchen, humming to herself as she goes. She returns a moment later with a towel over her shoulder, and carrying the wine and a corkscrew with two glasses. She places the wine and the glasses on top of the piano and the towel on the piano stool, then glances out to the harbour. A smile on her face tells us that she has seen and been seen by Evan. She moves up to the easel where she finds her portrait resting at the base. She picks it up and places it on the easel to study it*

After a second's pause Evan returns, soaked

Stella (*handing him the towel*) Here, take this.
Evan Thanks.

He removes his wet overcoat, which Stella takes

Stella I'll hang this to dry.

Stella exits, L

Evan sits on the stairs, drying his hair and neck. He looks at the portrait

Stella returns and stands behind him

What are you going to do with it?

Evan Don't know. What do you suggest I do with it?

Stella Put it away in the darkest cupboard you can find, where no-one will
ever see it.

Evan I'm sorry. I thought you liked it?

Stella I do. That's why I want you to put it away.

*Stella crosses to the piano to pick up the wineglasses, the bottle and the
corkscrew*

Evan Why did it make you cry?

Stella crosses to the table

Stella (*avoiding the issue*) I cry very easily. One of the first signs of
advancing middle age.

Evan You haven't answered my question.

Stella (*uncorking the bottle*) It isn't easy to answer. I think that ... perhaps
it reminded me suddenly of all the things that used to be. Or, perhaps it
would be truer to say the things that might have been.

Evan It didn't say that to me, when I was working on it.

Stella What did it say to you?

Evan It told me I wasn't painting the past at all. Only the present. Only the
things that are. Nothing is ever lost. Whatever you wanted once, or didn't
have; or whatever made you sad, or happy; it's all there in your eyes, in the
corner of your mouth, the lines on your forehead. When I worked on that
portrait, I wasn't painting the Stella of ten, twenty years ago. They don't
matter anymore. They've all finally merged into the complete person that
you are now. The Stella of today.

Stella (*with humility*) Is anyone ever final and complete?

Evan I think so. I think everyone reaches a moment when he or she stands
tall, and time stands still for about forty seconds. And in those "metamor-
phical" forty seconds, for the first, last and only time in their lives they are
both their complete selves. Then they fall and the decline sets in.

Stella How very depressing!

Evan Very.
Stella And rather above my head.

She hands him a glass of wine, indicating the conversation is over. They chink glasses and sip

Evan Mm. It's not bad, this.
Stella Last of a good vintage. The last of my pre-war cellar. We're down to the dregs of everything tonight. The wine, my scent; no more Nuits St Georges, no more *White Lilac*. And this dress isn't going to last much longer. The decline and fall of Stella Martyn.

They sip a while. Evan stands and stares at the picture. Stella perches on the arm of the chair

Evan I was wrong just now about this. It isn't the "final, complete Stella", after all. You've changed in the short time we've been here.
Stella Oh, new lines? More grey hairs?
Evan (*seriously*) Your eyes are darker than they were this afternoon, it's out-of-date already. A few hours ago, that was a bloody good portrait. It isn't good any longer.

He seizes the portrait and puts it, face against the wall, by the side of the piano

You're right, put it away in a dark cupboard.
Stella (*challenging him*) It is a good portrait! I only asked you to put it away because I don't want anyone else to see it.

Her confession is out before she has a chance to stop herself. Evan smiles, secretly satisfied, and moves downstage. Stella watches him, intrigued

Stella What's the matter?
Evan Nothing's the matter. I'm happy, that's all.
Stella Why, suddenly?
Evan Not suddenly. I've been happy all evening. But, especially now, because you feel the same way about it as I do. You see, I don't want anyone else to look at it either.

A pause. They look at each other. Evan turns out to look at the storm outside. Stella moves up to the piano stool, to break an awkward moment

Stella You've lost a button from your sleeve. I'll sew it on for you.

She pulls the stool downstage, trying to find enough light to begin sewing. She puts on her glasses. From inside the piano stool she removes a sewing wallet and proceeds to thread a needle. Evan drains his glass and moves up to her. Stella takes his wrist and rests her knee on the stool, to balance herself

(*As she sews*) You're very good about your clothes ... Cherry's quite hopeless, and when Jimmy's home I seem to be mending all the time ... Don't know why it is ... Suppose I must've brought them up badly ... they're both so untidy ...

Evan (*studying her closely*) Looking at you close up, I can see a million things I did wrong in that portrait. There's much more light in your hair, and you've got less chin than I thought.

Stella (*laughing*) How you managed to do any of it when I never sat for you once, I can't imagine.

Evan If you watch a face for two months and think of nothing else, you come to know it pretty well.

Stella I haven't been aware of you watching me.

Evan Haven't you?

Stella (*avoiding the question*) Anyway, I still don't know how you managed to find the time to do it.

Evan I've been getting up at half-past five every morning. Don't you remember saying I always seemed tired at breakfast? I've lost quite a bit of sleep one way and another.

Stella That was very foolish of you.

Evan (*mimicking her*) Very foolish.

Stella completes the sewing and cuts the loose thread off. She replaces the needle and scissors on the stool and then reaches across Evan to take his other sleeve

Stella There. Let's have a look at the other one, see if that's loose too ...

In one swift but easy movement, Evan removes her glasses and kisses her. We should see Stella give herself up to the kiss, almost trance-like, and get the feeling that it could progress. After a few seconds, Stella turns her head away

(*Softly*) Why did you do that? Just when we were so happy? You've spoilt everything.

Evan (*holding her hands*) What have I spoilt?

Stella Our being together, here in this house. All of us. You and me, and Cherry. Cherry!

*On speaking her daughter's name, Stella pulls herself off the stool and moves
L. Evan pursues her*

Evan (*reasonably*) We needn't bring Cherry into this. She hasn't anything
to do with you and me.

Stella What do you mean! She has *everything* to do with us.

Evan No! You say we're happy here. God, don't I know it! I've never been
so happy in my life. Because I've known there was a bond between us,
growing stronger every day. And you've known it too, deep in your heart,
but you won't admit it!

Stella Oh, but I do admit it.

Evan moves to embrace her once more. She stops him

Stella No! No, you don't understand. I can feel it all in my heart ... but I can't
explain it. From the very first evening I was happy; not only because of
Cherry, but because of you. And all these weeks it's grown stronger. The
things you said and the things you didn't say — even when we weren't
talking, when you just sat smoking a cigarette and I sat beside you, there
was something peaceful about it all. Now it isn't peaceful anymore.

Evan Why not? What I did was very simple. It's the thing that usually
happens between two people when they love each other.

Stella Evan! Don't pretend to be a child. You and I can't love each other in
that way.

Evan You say "that way", as if I'd done something repellent. There's only
one way to love and that's to give everything. Body, mind and heart. Well,
you can have all three of mine for what they're worth.

Stella You don't know what you're saying, or if you do then I refuse to listen
to you. For the first time since we've met, we're speaking a different
language.

Evan Are we? How?

Stella (*desperately*) I was brought up to respect morals. Standards. I respect
them still, I'll respect them all my life. Whatever I feel in my heart and in
my mind and in my body, those standards come first; like a rock in front
of every other feeling and every other sentiment. That's where we differ,
your generation and mine.

Evan My generation is no different from yours. Ten years? And all you say
about morals is false. False! You put up a defence, because you're afraid
of what might happen.

Stella I am not afraid! Fear has nothing to do with what I feel.

Evan Why didn't you push me away then when I kissed you? Why did you
stare at me with a lost look in your eyes? That wasn't self-righteous, that

wasn't moral. It was because the thing had happened that was bound to happen one day. (*He pleads with her*) I've loved you from the very first evening I came into this house. God knows! I didn't expect it, I didn't want it. But it's happened. There's no going back on it. God forgive me if I hurt you by telling you this, I have to tell you.

Stella You don't hurt me. I can cope with my own feelings. They don't matter.

Evan What matters then?

Stella (*loudly*) Cherry matters! And a basic knowledge of what's right and what's wrong. The deepest thing in any man or woman. You know that. You can't escape it. It's instinctive in every one of us.

Evan It isn't instinctive in me! My instinct tells me that during these past two months you've known in your heart that I was looking at you, and loving you and you were happy about it.

Stella (*turning away, not wanting to hear*) It isn't true!

Evan It is true!

Stella I won't have you say these things to me!

Evan (*pulling her close to him*) I *will* say them to you!

Through the storm outside, which is now at its strongest, we hear a muffled cry of "Help!" from the harbour. Evan lets go of Stella and rushes to the porch

(*Screaming out*) Hallo? What is it?

There is another muffled cry

All right, I'll see to it!

Evan moves up to the piano. He places Stella's glasses on top, then removes his jumper and his watch

(*For Stella's benefit*) It's the dinghy. It's come adrift.

Stella (*fearfully*) What are you going to do?

Evan Swim for it.

Stella You're not going to do anything of the sort! You must be mad. What does it matter? Let the boat sink!

Evan (*determinedly*) It won't take five seconds.

Stella (*grasping him, desperately*) Evan, no! It's dangerous. I won't let you go!

Evan seizes her arm, pulls himself free and glares at her maniacally

Evan Why? What do you care?

Evan charges out into the storm

Stella follows him to the porch, screaming after him

Stella Evan! Evan! ...

Stella stares out into the storm after him, struck with fear. As she stands an enormous thundercrack explodes overhead. She returns inside

Realizing what must be done, she exits L, *returning after a moment with a large towel*

As she re-enters another thunder crack explodes and the lights flicker on and off for a second, then fail completely, plunging the room into darkness. She rushes R *to try the light switch. The power is dead. With a quick glance towards the harbour she drops the towel on the armchair and then takes down two storm lanterns from a shelf over the stove. She places one, unlit, on the table,* L, *then moves across to the piano to place the second lamp on top of it. She proceeds to light it. A dim glow fills the room as the lamp is lit. She dashes back to the foot of the stage to search for Evan. She moves to the porch once more and screams down the slip to him*

Evan! Evan! ...

Evan comes running back in from the harbour, totally drenched from having dived into the sea

They embrace tightly on the porch, then return inside. Stella fetches the towel as Evan removes his wet shirt and his shoes, which he places at the bottom of the studio steps. Stella helps him dry himself off. Suddenly Evan grabs her, making her flinch

Evan (*intensely*) What would you have done if I hadn't come back, mm? Gone running up to the village for help?

Stella starts to cry

Or telephoned for the lifeboat? Perhaps they don't come out for single drowning men, only for ships' crews? (*He notices that she is crying and lets her go*)

She turns away from him

This is the second time today I've made you cry. Can you forgive me?

Stella (*trembling*) You frightened me. I know how the tide runs there, a man was drowned there doing the same thing. When you went out of the door I thought you were never coming back. Not because of the storm. I thought, for one terrible moment, that you wouldn't come back because of all the things I said to you.

Evan I wanted you to think that.

Stella (*annoyed*) That was cruel of you!

Evan I've told you before, I'm not the sort to make others happy.

Stella You've always made me happy, until now. Until tonight.

Evan This was supposed to be our special evening, wasn't it? Instead I make you cry. Can you forgive me?

Stella I forgive you everything. Except going down there on to the slip. I should have gone down into the water after you.

Evan Can you swim?

Stella No.

They realize the humour of the reply and Evan moves in closer to hold her in front of him

Never, never do it again.

Evan Do what?

Stella Dive into the harbour.

Evan (*turning her into him*) Now would be the moment to paint you. While you look like this, one tear still hovering in your eye.

There is a moment while they look at each other; possibly they are about to kiss again. The telephone rings. Evan moves across and answers it. Stella stares out into the remains of the storm

Hallo? Yes, Oh, OK. ... Yes. ... Bye. (*He holds the receiver in his hand and turns to Stella*) That was Cherry. She can't get back because of the storm, she's going to stop with Pam. The ferry isn't running any more tonight.

There is a final rumble of thunder. Stella turns out to the harbour once more. The Lights dim. Evan replaces the receiver

Black-out

ACT II

SCENE 1

The same. The following morning

Solo piano music — Satie — plays

In the half-light Evan enters slowly from the studio. He moves to the front of the stage and peers out over the harbour. After a moment he goes to the piano and picks up Stella's glasses. He moves across to his easel and picks up Stella's portrait, looks at it briefly, then exits back up the stairs with it. Mrs Tucket enters from the door, L, with a tray to collect the now empty wine bottle and glasses from last night. She also takes the towel left by the stove. As she crosses to the piano, Cherry enters from the door, R, obviously tired. She yawns

Cherry (*seeing Mrs Tucket*) Oh, morning.
Mrs Tucket Oh, morning, miss. You're down bright and early. Did the sunshine get you out of bed?
Cherry (*yawning*) No. I haven't been to bed.

Mrs Tucket looks at her, bewildered

Well, not in *this* house, at any rate.

Mrs Tucket is doubly bewildered

(*Explaining*) No, I got caught in it last night, so I spent the night with Pam.
Mrs Tucket Ah, well it did blow, and no mistake. I haven't known such a night for years. And the tide, so high. It washed right in under my door.
Cherry (*looking out to the harbour*) Well the dinghy seems to be all right. Evan must've pulled it up on to the slip. Any tea, Mrs T?
Mrs Tucket (*jumping to it*) I'll get you a cup straight 'way, miss. (*As she leaves*) I haven't been into your mother yet.

Mrs Tucket takes the full tray out with her and exits, L

Cherry (*calling after her*) Nothing to eat, thanks. Just a cup of tea.

Cherry moves up to the studio entrance and calls up to Evan

Evan!?

Evan, still dressing, comes down the stairs. He takes his shoes from the bottom step, where they were left last night

Evan Hallo. When did you get back?
Cherry Just a moment ago. (*She smiles*) Lovely evening, wasn't it? Did you get blown to bits up here?

Evan does not reply, but sits in the armchair and puts on his shoes and socks

Well, we had great fun. We went to *all* the pubs after the film and then came back and cooked kippers. Drank pints of beer. I've had indigestion ever since. So, what do you make of our West Country weather? Temperamental, isn't it?
Evan Very. Your dinghy came adrift. I had to go and rescue it.
Cherry How?
Evan Dived off the harbour into the slip and swam for it.
Cherry What a crazy thing to do! I wish I'd seen you. With a bit of luck we could've got that into the local paper; striking headlines. "Famous Artist Swept Away By Tide". You'd have had all the reporters on the doorstep.
Evan They'd be disappointed. The dinghy was firmly attached to the sea wall. Found out after I'd dived in.
Cherry Oh, that rather spoils it. I was picturing you half-way down the harbour, with Mother screaming after you like Bluebeard's wife! (*In her Mrs Tucket voice*) "If you'd got into that tide-way, you wouldn't be alive to tell the tale!"

Cherry's impression is interrupted by the return of Mrs Tucket, L. She brings a cup of tea

Mrs Tucket Here you are, miss. (*She sees Evan*) Oh, would you like a cup, Mr Davies?
Evan No thanks.
Mrs Tucket I went into your mother, miss. She said she hadn't any time for breakfast this morning. Said she had too much to do. She's had everything out of the linen cupboard — even the winter blankets.
Cherry (*to Evan*) She gets like that from time to time. We'll have to put a stop to it, or she'll have the whole house upside down.

Mrs Tucket (*eagerly*) Right you are, miss.

Mrs Tucket exits, R

Cherry looks out into the sunshine. Evan remains seated

Cherry It's going to be a lovely day. Who would believe that such an awful night could produce such a God-given morning? We ought to go for a picnic or something. Nothing much wrong with the dinghy ... full of rainwater, that's all.

Cherry moves out to stand on the porch

Stella enters from the door, R, *in an agitated and anxious mood. She speaks to Evan plainly*

Stella Where's Cherry?

Evan nods in the direction of the porch

Is she all right?
Evan (*calmly*) Perfectly. Any reason why she shouldn't be?
Stella No, none at all. Aren't you painting this morning?

Cherry, having heard voices, comes back into the room. Evan shakes his head in reply

Cherry Hallo, darling. Ooh, you look very domestic!
Stella How was your film? Did you enjoy it?
Cherry Well it wasn't Ingrid Bergman after all. What are you going to do, darling? Start on the storeroom when you've finished the linen cupboard?
Stella Very probably. I've got some telephoning to do.

Stella moves and picks up the receiver, trying the pips a few times

Cherry Oh, you can't telephone. There's about fifty lines down between here and Plymouth. And if you want any fish, there isn't any and the post's late. So, as far as the outside world's concerned, you've had it. (*She looks at them dubiously*) Awful atmosphere of gloom?

No response from them. Cherry moves towards the porch

Well, I suppose I'd better go and bail out the dinghy.

Evan (*jumping up*) I'll do it for you.

Cherry (*sharply*) Oh, that's very noble of you. Becoming boat-minded all of a sudden?

Evan exits to the harbour. After a pause, Cherry follows

Stella watches them leave then picks up the receiver again. Hearing no tone, she calls off

Stella Mrs Tucket? Mrs T?

Mrs Tucket enters, R

Mrs Tucket Did you call me, Mrs Martyn?

Stella (*impatiently*) Yes, the er ... the lines are down ... or something, and I must see Mr Hanson right away. Could you pop up the hill and ask him to come down and see me, as soon as he can?

Mrs Tucket Of course. I'll go at once.

Stella Thanks.

Mrs Tucket exits, R

Stella, still distracted, makes to leave and crosses to the door, R

Cherry enters from the porch

Cherry Well, I don't know what's come over Evan.

Stella Why?

Cherry Insisted on doing the boat himself, and sent me in to look after you. Very filial, I'm quite touched. (*She notices Stella's agitation*) What's the matter, darling? You look awfully preoccupied.

Stella Nothing's the matter. I must go and tidy up. Robert's coming down.

Cherry Ah, Robert. He's very aloof these days. I think Pam must be right.

Stella (*quickly*) Right? What about?

Cherry Well, according to her, and other people, Robert doesn't come here anymore because he dislikes Evan.

Stella Oh how stupid!

Cherry I agree. And even if it is true, I couldn't care less. Robert's your property, not mine.

Cherry moves, about to leave. Stella prevents her

Stella I've got to talk to you, darling, very seriously, for a moment.

Cherry Oh dear. What about?

Stella About ... about you ... and Evan. It's not right for us all to live here together; you two ought to be on your own.

Cherry Don't be ridiculous!

Stella I'm not being ridiculous, I'm right. I've known it for some time.

Cherry But we love being here, and being with you. Evan's a different person from who he was. He's happy and well, and he scarcely touches the whisky. And he's doing good work, you don't know how good.

Stella Yes, I do. But it would be better work, and happier for you both if you had the place to yourselves ——

Cherry But ——

Stella — I'm talking plain, common sense. Living with relations is all very well, for a time. But eventually, a man needs to feel he's living in his own home. Not just a guest in someone else's. I know how you and Evan love it here. But you'd love it so much more if it belonged to you and you had the place to yourselves.

Cherry (*utterly lost*) I ... I don't understand. Why bring this up now, out of the blue? Just when we're all so happy.

Stella Well, that's just it. Are we all happy?

Cherry Yes. I thought we were. (*She is suddenly struck*) You both looked strange just now. What's Evan been saying to you? If he's been rude or unkind, I'll never forgive him!

Cherry starts for the porch and Stella goes to stop her

Stella No! He hasn't been rude or unkind. All this has been at the back of my mind for weeks now. The storm last night seemed to bring it all close; I lay awake and thought about you both, but at the same time, I thought about myself. If it's not right for you and Evan to live here with me, neither is it right for me to live here with you. (*She faces Cherry*) Cherry, what would you say if I told you I'd made up my mind to marry Robert?

Cherry (*not knowing whether to laugh or cry*) Oh! Mother?!

Stella (*sternly*) Why not? Yes, I know we've always joked about it. The "routine" proposal, we've been unjust and unfair.

Cherry (*very concerned*) You've never talked like this before. The times you've laughed about Robert and that dreary bloody house of his! You'd go mad if you lived up there.

Stella (*protesting*) The house is charming, and so's the garden. Neglected, that's all. And anyway, he's my generation. We understand each other.

Cherry Are you going to tell him all this, when he comes down here?

Stella (*determinedly*) Probably. Why?
Cherry (*wildly*) All right then. Go ahead. Make an arse of yourself! It's not for your only daughter to stop you!
Stella Cherry!
Cherry (*sharply*) What!?

There is a second's pause

Stella (*quietly*) Nothing.

Stella exits, R

Cherry stands, quite confused at this news. Realizing the full impact of the possible marriage, she moves to the porch and calls out to Evan

Cherry Evan! Come here, I want you!

Evan enters from the harbour, cautious of her obvious distress

Evan (*speaking as he enters*) What's the matter?
Cherry (*firmly*) What's wrong with Mother?
Evan What d'you mean?
Cherry Did you get in a mood last night? Mm? Sulk or get drunk or something?
Evan (*covering*) I did not.
Cherry Then what the hell's happened to her then? She's been talking about clearing off and leaving the house to us. Says she's not happy here and that we ought to have the place to ourselves. And she wants to marry Robert.
Evan (*to himself*) God!
Cherry She was perfectly all right yesterday. Has she gone mad or something? (*She becomes tearful*) If she goes and lays herself at his door, through some mistaken idea of helping us ... I don't know what I'd do. She's the only one who matters — (*she brushes away a tear*) except you. I know I tease her, but she knows I love her!
Evan (*beginning to understand the reality of it all*) You've never spoken like this before. Not to me. I thought you took Stella for granted? You show your affection in an odd way, you know.
Cherry (*through her tears*) I'm ... I'm not very good at telling people when I love them; it's always been my trouble.
Evan (*abruptly*) Has it? (*In a frustrated and helpless mood, he moves to the piano and pours himself a large whisky*)
Cherry Bit early for that, isn't it?

Evan Much too early!

Cherry I'd have some myself if it didn't make me feel so sick. I feel lousy anyhow, and my face wants washing.

Evan (*automatically*) It always does!

Cherry glares at him

Cherry Well that's one good thing about our marriage, Evan. No false sentiment. (*She loses control again*) We know exactly where we are with each other ... We could have been married for years!

She can hold back her tears no longer and moves in to him, for support. She holds him tightly, he holds her dispassionately

Christ, Evan! What are we going to do?

Evan (*over her shoulder*) I don't know.

Mrs Tucket and Robert are heard (ad lib) in the hall, off R

Mrs Tucket (*off*) You go straight on in, sir. I think Mrs Martyn's in there ....

Robert (*off*) Oh, thank you, Mrs Tucket. Lovely night wasn't it ...?

Cherry (*simultaneously; letting go of Evan*) God! There's Robert. I can't face him, I'll only say something tactless. You'll have to deal with him.

Cherry exits up to the studio, pulling the door to as she goes

Evan, preparing to face Robert, pours himself another drink

Robert enters, R. *He sees Evan's glass. There is immediate tension between the two men*

Robert Oh. Morning.

Evan (*over-brightly*) Morning!

Pause

Robert Lovely night, wasn't it?

Evan Mm!

Another silence

Robert Did the er, did the rain come into the studio?

Evan (*sarcastically*) Well if it did, I didn't notice it. (*He indicates his glass*)
Robert (*ignoring him*) Used to, when I used the attic as a sail-loft.
Evan (*mocking*) I didn't know you ever used the attic.
Robert Didn't you? Well, you forget, I've known the family for over fifteen
  years.
Evan (*insultingly*) No, I don't! I remember only too well. It gives you great
  advantage over everybody else, doesn't it? (*He offers Robert the bottle*)
  Whisky?
Robert (*gritting his teeth*) No, thank you. I've just had breakfast.
Evan So did I!

Evan pours himself another drink then moves away from the piano to look
hard at Robert

  You know, I've been a fool these past weeks, living off fruit and lemonade.
  Whisky is the only drink for a man of my temperament. Even at ten in the
  morning. It settles the stomach, steadies the nerves and makes you say
  damn all to the woman you love! (*He downs the drink*) Ahh! You know,
  I sometimes think that you and I are very much alike.
Robert (*scoffing*) Can't say the thought has ever struck me. In fact, I can't
  think of two people *less* alike.
Evan (*more seriously*) Not on the surface, no. But inside, when it comes to
  fundamentals, yes. We both keep our emotions under control and once our
  choice has been made, where our affections are concerned, we both remain
  constant. Forever.
Robert (*smiling at him*) A very pretty speech. Though exactly what it refers
  to, I've no idea.
Evan (*withdrawing*) No? Forget it then. It doesn't matter one way or the
  other.

Stella enters, L, carrying a bowl of grapes. She immediately sees the two
men and senses the tense atmosphere

  Ah! How extremely appropriate! The lady of the house, in question;
  bearing in her hands, Robert, a bunch of grapes! For you, of course. (*He*
  passes Robert the bottle) Give Stella some whisky, Robert.
Robert (*ignoring him*) I believe you wanted to see me about something,
  Stella? Perhaps it would be more convenient if I called back some other
  time?
Evan (*loudly*) Much more convenient! We're all very busy at the moment,
  turning out the linen cupboard!

Stella slams the plate down on to the table and crosses to Robert

Robert (*with growing anger*) If it's impossible for you to have any privacy here, Stella, perhaps it would be safer for you to come up to my house. That is, if the business is urgent?

Stella It is rather urgent ——

Evan Oh, come, come! Surely it can't be as urgent as all that? After all, you've waited ten years to come to a decision. Surely an hour or so, one way or the other, won't kill you!

Robert (*to Stella*) Is Cherry at home? Because if she is, it mightn't be a bad idea if she persuaded him to lie down. (*Aloud to Evan*) He appears to be suffering from a hangover!

Evan (*smugly*) Oh, not a hangover old boy! I'm still in very good form. (*Threatening*) I shan't start knocking anyone's head off, not for another twenty-four hours, at least!

Robert (*furiously*) You know, the services taught me a method that would be very effective with you, young man!

Robert draws back his fist as if about to move and strike Evan. Stella intervenes and keeps the men apart. Evan swaggers, challenging Robert to hit him

Stella (*holding Robert*) No, Bob!

Evan Ho, ho! Did they really, Bob? I never discovered it. What did they use? Hypnosis, or yoga; or a dash of both? You see, Bob, I really do want to be cured. I've tried everything. Lemon and glucose, eating raw liver, breathing deeply in front of an open window. Nothing works!

Robert (*restraining himself*) I shall be at home all day, if you need me Stella. You and Cherry had better come up for lunch. (*He moves to the door, R, and turns back*) And if you've got any more of that stuff in the house, you'd be wise to lock it away!

Robert leaves, slamming the door

Stella turns furiously to Evan. He now drops all pretence of being drunk

Stella How *dare* you behave like this in my house!

Evan Sorry. I had to get rid of him somehow. There was no other way.

Stella You're not drunk at all!

Evan It takes more than a few whiskies to do that. Course I'm not drunk. Anyway, it worked. You're not going to speak to Robert alone.

Stella (*contemptuously*) What makes you think I want to?

Evan Cherry told me. You were going to ask him to marry you!

Stella And why not?

Evan You don't love *him*. And you never will!

Stella (*defensively*) Robert has loved me faithfully and devotedly for years. You told me I was lonely. You're right, I am lonely. By marrying Robert I'll make sure that I am not lonely in the future.

Evan It's no use and it won't work. Not that sort of lie.

Stella (*desperately*) *I'm not lying.* I'm telling the truth.

Evan There's not a word of truth in anything you've said. Your whole body is a lie. The back of your head, your shoulders, your hands. I know exactly what's happened to you. I knew exactly how it would be when I said goodnight and let you go. Up went the barriers. God! Why does the morning have to do this to you? Look at me!

Stella Evan! I can't go on living in this house with you and Cherry. Not after the things we said last night.

Evan The things we said last night will be forgotten. I love you well enough for that. It'll be something that never happened. You don't believe me?

Stella I do believe you. I believe you have a stronger will than I possess myself. You could go on living here and everything seem just as it was. I can't do that. I'm not made that way.

Evan I don't understand.

Stella (*softly and intensely*) No! Your generation don't understand.

Evan (*trying to comprehend*) You'd throw away all friendship, all loyalty, all affection; throw it all away because of the things I told you? Things you didn't want to hear.

Stella moves away from him, her eyes now full of tears

Stella (*barely audible*) But that's just it ... I did want to hear them. That's what's made me treacherous and disloyal. I looked in the glass just now. The sunlight was very merciless. The true Stella looked me in the face. That's when you should have finished your portrait.

Evan (*frustrated*) Who is the true Stella?

Stella Someone selfish... and hard. (*This is her first true admission*) Someone who, in a few hours, has grown jealous of her own daughter.

Evan What are you trying to tell me?

Stella (*unsure herself*) Everything ... nothing. All I know is that the world has become a different place. I feel bewildered and lost, in a desperate sort of way. Not a way I understand.

Evan moves to touch her. She holds up her hands to stop him

Evan Darling.

Stella No! No. You see, we're both different people from the ones we were yesterday.

Evan Perhaps we are. But, if you believe that, can you still marry Robert? Can you?

The front doorbell rings. They both stare at each other, not having heard it

After a second, Cherry comes down the studio stairs. She looks at them both, uncertainly, but still aware they are having more than a simple talk. She moves off the stairs

Cherry Shall I go?

There is no definite response to the question. She sighs and leaves, R

Stella and Evan remain silent in the room for a few moments. Evan makes a slight move to Stella, as if about to speak

Cherry returns with a telegram

Cherry (*to Stella*) Telegram, for you. (*She hands the telegram to Stella*) The boy's waiting for an answer.

Stella (*suddenly alert*) Telegram? Who from? What about?

Cherry (*snapping*) I don't know! You'd better open it and see.

Stella moves across to the piano to take her glasses from their usual place. She cannot see them

Stella What did I do with my glasses?

Evan They're up in the studio. And you don't need them. Not in this "merciless sunlight".

Stella opens the envelope and reads

Cherry Well? Anything exciting?

Stella (*reading*) It's from Jimmy. ... His ship arrived in Plymouth last night ... he's had some sort of accident ... his foot, or something. ... He's broken it! He says he's coming home today on sick-leave!

Cherry Typical of Jimmy! Always turns up, just when he's not wanted.

Stella (*protectively*) He is wanted! He's always wanted.

Cherry Hm, the lost lamb returned to the fold?

Evan Don't you want to send a message back, Stella? The boy's waiting.
Stella What? Oh. Yes, of course. (*To Evan*) Have you got a pencil?
Evan I'll write it for you. What do you want to say?
Stella Er ... put, "Your room ready, as always". ... And sign it, "Mother".

Stella turns to Cherry for some kind of reassurance. Evan writes the reply

The Lights snap to a Black-out

The action is continuous. A traditional jazz recording plays. The Lights rise on the following cross-over to SCENE 2:

Mrs Tucket enters R, *and helps Jimmy Martyn to hobble on, with his walking-stick. She is carrying a newspaper. His left foot is bandaged, not yet plastered. Stella exits,* L. *Evan exits up to the studio*

Cherry pulls the armchair DL, *leaving a passage behind it and the table. She takes a footstool from beside the stove and a cushion from the sofa and sets them in front of the chair as a support for Jimmy's foot*

Mrs Tucket collects Cherry's teacup from the table, puts the newspaper down and exits, L

The Lights fade

SCENE 2

Six hours later

The Lights come up to reveal Jimmy sitting in the armchair. He is eighteen, chirpy but often tactless. His foot is propped on the footstool and supported with a cushion. He has a glass of beer. He and Cherry are playing a mock-game of cricket, with Cherry bowling an imaginary ball and Jimmy striking it with his walking stick. The radio, on the table, is playing at full blast

Jimmy SIX! Yes! Look, it's not a question of looks at all. It's the way they move, the way they smile, the way they set out to please. I tell you, English women don't begin to compare with Americans.
Cherry (*groaning*) Oh, "Join the Navy and see the world"?
Jimmy I'm not joking, I'm serious. The whole feminine outlook on life is different once you get across the Atlantic. (*Coyly*) You don't seem to realize what happens when chaps like us go ashore there.

Cherry Huh, yes I do! You call it showing the flag and it costs the British taxpayer millions.

Jimmy You're just jealous because you've never been out of England. Did I tell you the one about the Scotsman and the submarine?

Cherry Yes, you did. And I don't want to hear it again.

Jimmy Well, there's an even funnier one about an old woman, a bottle of brandy and a cockatoo!

Cherry (*snatching his stick and making to whack his foot*) Shut up! Mother'll hear you!

Jimmy Ow! Sod this foot! (*He grovels*) Cherry, I feel like a beer.

Cherry Well shout for one then.

Jimmy (*sulking*) Oh, I'm going to love this! Lying around like an old cripple for God-knows how long!

Cherry stands over him with his walking-stick in the air, like an executioner about to cut off his foot

(*Quickly*) DON'T! (*He shouts off for assistance*) Mother!

Stella (*off*) Coming, darling.

Jimmy (*shouting*) Get me another beer will you? And some more cigarettes.

Stella enters R, trying to hear over the noise of the radio music

Stella What?

Jimmy Some more beer and a packet of cigarettes. Where have you been for the last hour?

Stella (*moving L*) Oh, seeing to a hundred and one things, darling. Mrs Tucket goes home midday on Saturdays. I'll get you a beer.

Cherry Bring two glasses, I'll have one too.

Stella (*passing behind the chair to the radio*) Anyone mind if I turn this off? (*She does so*) It's making a terrible racket.

She exits L

Jimmy (*calling after her*) Sorry. Didn't notice. Bloody good tune, I think.

Stella returns with the beer and glasses

Stella (*handing Jimmy a glass and a beer*) Yes, well I'm sure I'll hear it later.

She moves across to Cherry, who is now standing on the studio stairs, looking up to the attic

(*Handing her a beer and a glass*) Darling?
Jimmy Why don't you have one? Do you good!
Stella No, I don't want any.
Jimmy (*cheekily*) Afraid of putting on weight?
Stella (*nudging him, amused*) No, I'm not! How's your foot?
Jimmy Lousy. Can't you loosen the bandage or something?
Stella Dr Wood will be here soon. He'll do it for you properly.
Jimmy (*making a baby face; pleading*) He won't. He'll make it a hundred
  times worse, they always do.

Stella concedes and sits on the edge of the stool to study the knotted bandage

*From the studio, Evan enters, now semi-formally dressed in his Act I suit.
He moves to the piano and picks up a telegram, which he reads. Cherry
watches him, but they do not exchange glances yet*

Ow! Careful.
Stella (*fumbling with the knot*) Sorry, darling. I can't see to do the knot.
Jimmy Got your glasses?
Stella No.

*She remembers the last time she wore them — last night sewing Evan's
sleeve. Evan overhears this and, unseen by all, except Stella, takes them from
his trouser pocket. Cherry moves behind the armchair and is teasing Jimmy
about having a larger glass of beer than his. Neither of them see Stella move
to the piano and quietly collect her glasses from Evan. Evan and Stella
exchange a brief glance*

(*Putting on her glasses and returning to the stool*) Now then, let's have a
proper look.

She squints and unties the knot

Evan, seeing her in her dutiful role of mother, exits upstairs

Cherry watches him go, hoping for a reaction

Jimmy Ouch!
Stella Sorry. Yes, it is a bit tight. (*She loosens it*) Is that any better?
Jimmy A bit. Thanks.

Stella stands, about to leave. Jimmy pulls her down on to his lap and holds her there

Now come on, sit down a minute! I've hardly spoken to you all day.

Stella Darling, that's not fair! I played backgammon with you for two hours after lunch.

Jimmy Yes, and very distracted you were too. Didn't know what you were doing half the time.

Stella Well, I forget how to play when you're away so much.

Jimmy Get Evan to give you a game, when I'm not here. He's terrific. Thrashed me before tea. (*He calls over to the piano, expecting to see Evan*) Didn't you, Evan? Oh. Where's he gone?

Cherry (*moving down to the armchair*) Upstairs. Brooding over his pictures, I expect.

Jimmy Oh. Don't you "brood" with him?

Cherry Not me. You don't know my husband. Independent type.

Jimmy Well, you haven't picked too badly.

The family are now grouped around the armchair. Jimmy is sitting, Stella is on his lap and Cherry, upstage of them, leans over the back of the chair

What do you think of your new son-in-law, Mother?

Stella (*reaching across for Cherry's arm*) I'm very fond of him.

Cherry You ought to see Evan and Mother in the evenings. Very pre-war! Evan sits at the piano, playing waltzes, and Mother just sits, looking sentimental!

Jimmy (*mimicking*) "Oh, how absolutely wizard!" Will you give us a show tonight, Mother? I feel like a good cry!

Jimmy and Cherry giggle. Stella stands, uneasily

Oh, Christ! Now I've set her on the move again! How's the boyfriend, darling?

Stella (*turning sharply*) What do you mean?

Jimmy Oh, don't be coy! Robert, of course. Has he popped the question lately?

Cherry nudges him in the back. Jimmy looks surprised

Stella (*moving* R) Will you see the doctor here? Or in your room?

Jimmy (*confused*) Er ... in my room ... The light's better in there. He can peel off the bandages and have a proper squint!

Stella Well, I'll get some towels and see that the water's hot.
Jimmy No hurry.
Stella (*moving to the door,* R) No. I'd rather do it now. Get it over and done
with.

She exits and closes the door behind her

*Jimmy looks bemused for a second, then reaches behind him and switches the
radio back on at full blast*

Jimmy Christ! What's up with her?
Cherry (*turning the radio down*) I was going to tell you, but there hasn't been
a chance.
Jimmy Mm?
Cherry There's a hell of a drama going on with Robert at the moment.
Jimmy What's happened? Have they fallen out?
Cherry I wish to God they had. (*Confidentially*) She says she's going to
marry him.
Jimmy No! What suddenly? Without any reason?
Cherry No reason at all. Except she thinks that Evan and I ought to have the
place to ourselves. That it's "wrong for us all to be here together".
Jimmy Well they get on, don't they?
Cherry Who?
Jimmy Evan and Mother.
Cherry Oh, yes. Terrific buddies. Being here has been perfect. Everything
dead easy. Of course, we have to remember that Evan's an outsider. He
doesn't understand Mother like we do.
Jimmy (*affecting maturity*) No, course.
Cherry Men are so bloody selfish! If Robert's been going on about being
lonely, and how he can't live without her — well, she's so soft-hearted,
she'd fall for it at once. If she thought she was making anyone unhappy,
she couldn't bear it. She'd feel she'd committed a crime.
Jimmy (*worldly-wise*) That's the trouble with her generation. They always
take everything so bloody seriously.
Cherry I know. Fatal. Why can't they behave more like us?
Jimmy (*thinking*) I suppose that seeing you and Evan together hasn't made
her, well, you know ... feel out of things? Sounds silly, but you know what
I mean.
Cherry Well, that doesn't add up. I mean, Evan and I are so matter of fact.
Jimmy Great relief, I should think.
Cherry Yeh.
Jimmy Ah, it's always embarrassing being in a house where two people have

just got married. (*Teasing*) They look at each other all the time, have those private little jokes ...

Cherry Mother's different. The closer people are, the happier she becomes.

Jimmy (*energetically, dismissing the subject*) Well it's no use getting morbid about it. If she starts talking to me about Robert, I'll just tease her like mad. See what effect that has!

Cherry I don't think she could take it at the moment. She's got that look behind her eyes, like the slightest thing will make her cry.

Jimmy Well the only thing to do is to keep her busy and cheerful! Games every evening and lots to do all day. Fun and roars of laughter from morning till night. (*He reaches behind him and turns the radio up, full volume*) You leave it to me!

Cherry It won't work.

Jimmy It's *got* to work! We can't have her walking off and marrying Robert. What the hell would happen to me?

Cherry (*amused*) Selfish little sod! The whole point is what's going to happen to her?

Evan calls down from the studio. Cherry moves across and stands at the bottom step

Evan (*off*) Cherry! Is that telephone working yet?

Cherry (*calling back up*) I don't know. I'll try it.

She crosses to the telephone and lifts the receiver to test it

Turn that down, will you?

Jimmy (*defiantly*) No!

Cherry (*threatening*) Turn it down!

Jimmy reluctantly turns the radio down

Hallo? Operator? Hallo? ... No, you're very faint ... is it clear yet? ... Oh, right. ... Thank you. (*She hangs up and crosses back to the studio stairs. She calls up*) The men are still working on the line. They'll give us a ring as soon as it's OK. It won't be long now.

Evan (*off*) Thanks.

Cherry Did you want me to get through to someone for you?

Evan (*off*) No, don't bother. It doesn't matter.

Jimmy Cherry, as you're up, go and tell Mother I will have spaghetti and cheese for supper, after all. With some tomato sauce — she knows the kind I mean.

Cherry Such a pig! (*In her Mrs Tucket voice*) "Anythin' else, sir?"

Jimmy Yes. Tell her to open that last bottle of burgundy.

Cherry (*crossing behind the chair*) Saw the empty in the dustbin this morning. So, you've had it!

She picks up the newspaper from the table and smacks him with it before she goes out, L

Jimmy snatches the newspaper from her and begins reading through it

Evan enters from the studio and gives Jimmy a playful tap on the head

Evan How's the foot?

Jimmy Awful! It'll be worse when the quack has a go at it.

Evan crosses to the piano and looks for his telegram

Evan Ah, fill yourself full of whisky. You won't feel a thing.

Jimmy Don't worry. I've got some rum upstairs, real stuff. Straight from Jamaica. Like some?

Evan Er, no. I don't think so. Not at the moment.

Evan sits on the piano stool

Jimmy What have you been doing up there?

Evan Going through some old pictures. Sorting out the ones for export, and throwing the rest out.

Jimmy Sounds very business-like and commercial. What do you do with the duds?

Evan Send them to the Royal Academy.

They both laugh

Jimmy (*after a pause*) I wish you'd paint my portrait one day.

Evan Perhaps I will. But not till you're First Sea Lord. It wouldn't pay me.

Jimmy I suppose it must be odd being an artist. Seeing things in people's faces that others can't see at all.

Evan Yes, sometimes.

Jimmy All kinds of hidden thoughts and feelings. (*He shivers*) Err! It's a bit creepy when you come to think of it.

Evan Perhaps.

Jimmy I remember once, when I was a kid, I did a drawing of a ship. I thought it was pretty good; and then my father asked to look at it, and I felt so ashamed I went out and chucked it on the bonfire.

Evan Very wise of you. (*He is struck with an idea*) I've never thought of that.

Jimmy (*encouraging him*) We could have a bonfire with all your throw-outs.

Evan We could. Would you enjoy it?

Jimmy It'd make a good blaze!

Evan jumps up and exits to the studio

Jimmy gives an excited and self-satisfied gesture

Evan returns, tearing a canvas from its frame. He pauses on the stairs for a second

Stella enters, R

Evan This isn't exactly a throw-out. It's too personal for export, and too good for the Royal Academy.

Evan moves behind the armchair, switches off the radio and stops near the stove

Jimmy Let's have a look at it!

Evan shields it from Jimmy

Oh, show me. It's a woman, isn't it?

Evan It is.

Stella and Evan exchange a look. We know now that it is the portrait of Stella

Jimmy (*raunchy*) Cor! Naked and unashamed!

Evan No. Clothed and in her right mind. (*He moves towards the stove*)

Stella Did you ever love her?

Evan (*looking towards Stella*) I'll love her all my life.

Jimmy Good for you! Personally, I don't know what you see in Cherry myself, but ...

Evan (*cutting in*) Cherry? ... (*Guarded*) Oh, yes.

He tears the canvas from its frame, lifts the lid of the stove and throws the canvas into the flames. A glow of light flickers

Stella No! Oh, no! (*She crosses to the armchair, but is too late to stop Evan. Softly*) Why?
Jimmy (*raucously*) He's completely mad!! Might've made money that!
Evan I wouldn't want it to.
Jimmy Well, there she burns. A masterpiece, lost to the world.

The front doorbell rings

Stella There's the doctor.
Cherry (*off*) I'll go!
Jimmy (*with dread*) Oh, give us a hand up.

Evan helps Jimmy to his feet

I warn you if he hurts me, I'll scream the place down. (*He hobbles to the door, then turns back*) Hope he's careful. (*In a Biggles voice*) "I'm one of those boys that hurts easily!" (*He chuckles to himself*)

Jimmy exits

Evan and Stella are silent for a moment

Stella Why did you burn it?
Evan You know why.
Stella You could have given it to me.
Evan No. The day might come when you'd have shared it with someone else. With Robert, if you're going to marry him.
Stella That'll never happen.
Evan Are you sure?
Stella Quite sure.
Evan How do you know?
Stella Does it matter?
Evan (*passionately*) It does to me.

A slight pause. Stella considers her explanation

Stella When I couldn't find my glasses just now, I remembered that the last time I wore them was last night — sewing your sleeve. And, then, when you gave them back to me ... something in your look. I knew I could never marry Robert.
Evan I've made up my mind about the future too.
Stella Whose future?

Evan Cherry's, and yours. And mine.

Stella What are you going to do?

Evan The only thing I can do. Go away from here.

Stella Do you mean, go away to live? Taking Cherry with you?

Evan Isn't that what you want me to do?

Stella (*eagerly*) Yes. And you'll look after her, and make her happy?

Evan I'll try. You're the only one who matters, to both of us. I don't know who loves you most. Cherry or me. Funny, isn't it? Seeing you with Jimmy this afternoon reminded me of all sorts of things I hadn't thought about for years. It hurt at first. But I won't let it hurt anymore. I'd like you to be proud of me one day. Do something that'll make you feel all this has been worth while.

Stella Oh, I am proud of you now. Not of your painting. That'll always be a part of me. I'm proud because you've decided alone; without my asking. It'll be New York, won't it?

Evan Yes.

Stella It'll be exciting for Cherry. A new life, a new world. Seeing things she's never seen before. (*A pause*) When you do decide to go away from here, let's have no farewells, no last moments, no waving goodbye across the harbour.

Evan (*putting his hand on his heart*) I promise.

Stella And you'll have to apologize to Robert, you know. He thinks you're heading for d.t.'s.

Evan He wouldn't be far wrong. I probably shall be heading for the d.t.'s, on the other side of the Atlantic.

Stella If you did it'd break my heart.

Evan Would it?

Stella Yes. (*She changes the subject*) I wish I didn't have to stay up with Jimmy tonight. I'd like to go to bed very early, and sleep right through until late tomorrow morning. I'm so tired.

Evan (*taking her hands*) I want to kiss you.

Stella (*softly*) Do you?

They look at each other intently. We feel that they may be about to kiss. Their moment is broken by Jimmy shouting from off

Jimmy (*off*) Mother!

Stella turns, uncertain what to do. Evan releases her hands and instructs her

Evan All right. Go to him.

Stella smiles, then moves to the door, R. She pauses briefly at the door. Evan indicates for her to go

   Stella exits

Evan stands frozen for a second. The telephone rings. He crosses to answer it

Evan Hallo? Is it clear? ... Then I want Penzance, one-seven-o. ... Thank you, I'll hold.

Evan waits. He looks out of the right door, to make sure no-one is listening

   Hallo? Is that Western Union? Er, my name is Evan Davies. I sent a cable to New York yesterday morning. ... That's right. ... Good. Well, I want to send another one cancelling the one I sent yesterday. ... Yes. Put "Accept your offer — going to London tonight. Will make all arrangements there". Thank you. That's all. (*He replaces the receiver*)

A ferry hoots and he crosses downstage to stare out to the harbour for a moment

Suddenly, he turns and darts up the stairs

Cherry enters, L. She crosses to the telephone and picks up the receiver

Evan returns, carrying his suitcase and suit jacket

Cherry Um, I thought I heard the telephone?
Evan (*putting his suitcase on the porch*) You did. It was for me.
Cherry Anything important?
Evan Very important. I've got to catch the night-train to London.
Cherry (*worried*) Why? What for? ... Sorry.
Evan What about?
Cherry Our arrangement when we married. Never to ask each other questions.
Evan Takes a bit of doing sometimes. I don't make a very satisfactory husband, do I?
Cherry I wouldn't want you any different.
Evan I can't think of any other person who'd put up with me.
Cherry Well that's very lucky, from my point of view.
Evan I've decided to accept that offer from New York.

Cherry is dumbfounded. He calms her

Now, it means loads of work, different from anything I've done before. Will you come?

Cherry You know I will! Oh, Evan! That's wonderful!

They embrace

Evan Not a word to anyone, you understand. This is our secret.

Cherry nods

I'll telephone you tomorrow evening from London when I've found out more about it. There'll be lots to do — packing and so on. And our seats to book. You can follow on with our things in a day or two.

Cherry (*still absorbing it*) It's so exciting! I thought you refused the offer and didn't want to go?

Evan Did you? You should've known me better. (*He puts his jacket on*) Our marriage has been strange so far, hasn't it?

Cherry (*not wanting to go into it now*) I don't think so.

Evan You're very loyal.

Cherry (*looking out to the harbour*) It'll be a hell of a wrench leaving here, for both of us. But it'll be worth it. You're going to do better work than ever before, in New York.

Evan Oh? What makes you think that?

Cherry What Mother would call "intuition".

Evan (*moving up to the piano to get a pencil and notepaper*) Stella and I were talking about this, before the cable came. I told her that one of these days I'd be out of this house and she wouldn't know I'd gone. I bet her five quid I could do it. I'm going to write my goodbyes and leave them on the piano. She'll think it's a great joke.

Cherry Are you sure? Not much of a joke.

Evan (*writing*) She'll understand.

Cherry You know, Evan. I've just suddenly thought. If we go away from here, Mother'll have the house to herself again, won't she? Well, except for Jimmy.

Evan She will.

Cherry Were you thinking of her when the cable came?

Evan (*folding the note and leaning it against a glass*) I was thinking of you both.

Offstage we hear the doctor leaving and voices. The ferry hoots again

Cherry There's the doctor. You'd better hurry or you'll run into everybody.
Evan (*moving to porch*) Come across the ferry with me and put me in the train. (*He picks up his suitcase*) And will you do one more thing for me?
Cherry Anything, darling.
Evan Stay up with Jimmy tonight.
Cherry Is that all? Course!
Evan Come on!

They exit to the harbour, hurriedly

A moment passes. The door R opens and Jimmy limps back in followed by Stella. He makes for the armchair

Jimmy Thank God that's over!
Stella Come on, darling! He didn't hurt you. Sit down and let me prop up the cushions for you.

Stella rearranges the chair cushions and Jimmy sits. Stella hands him the newspaper

There. Better? Want a drink?
Jimmy Not at the moment. I'll wait till supper. Six weeks he said I'll be here with this useless foot! What am I going to do all the time?
Stella Oh, don't worry. We'll think of something. Backgammon, day and night.

Stella collects the empty beer glasses and bottles and takes them off, L

Jimmy reads

Stella returns

Jimmy Where's Evan? Tell him to come and cheer me up.
Stella He's in the studio I expect. I'll call him.

Stella moves behind the chair and as she gets to the studio door we hear the sharp whistle of the ferry horn. Stella looks round quickly. She sees the note left on the piano and slowly crosses to collect it, knowing full well what it will say. She begins to read it

Jimmy (*suddenly*) I'll tell you what we'll do tonight. We'll have a riot! Yes!
  And lots of music.

He turns the radio on. A traditional recording of "Red Sails in the Sunset"
begins to play

  Evan can thump the piano, and I'll play all those old records you like.
  You'd like that, sweetheart, wouldn't you?

Stella finishes reading and moves slowly DR. *She stares out*

  What are you doing, darling?

The Lights begin to fade down to a solo spot on Stella

Stella Watching the ferry.
Jimmy What's it doing?
Stella It's half-way across the harbour already. In a moment it'll reach the
  other side.

Stella is now standing in a pool of light. She watches out for a moment longer,
then, as the Lights fade, she crumples the note in her hand

The music continues and the Lights fade to Black-out

FURNITURE AND PROPERTY LIST

ACT I

SCENE 1

On stage: Sofa with cushions
Armchairs
Piano. *On it:* drinks tray with glasses, pencil and notepaper
Piano stool. *In it:* sewing wallet with thread, needle and scissors
Table. *On it:* Radio
Stove
Local newspaper
Shelf. *On it:* 2 storm lanterns, matches
Telephone
Footstool

Off stage: Whisky bottle (**Robert**)
Outdoor shoes (**Mrs Tucket**)
Basket (**Mrs Tucket**)
Luggage, rucksack. *In it:* whisky bottle (**Evan**)
Paint box. *In it:* paint, brushes, rags, etc. (**Evan**)
Easel, pallet, canvasses and portraits, etc., painting apron (**Evan**)
Whisky bottle (**Stella**)
Roses (**Stella**)
Vase (**Stella**)
Blankets, sheets and pillows (**Stella** and **Cherry**)
Three dinner-napkins and rings (**Stella**)

Personal: **Robert:** watch

SCENE 2

Off stage: Basket and cardigan (**Mrs Tucket**)
Sailing gear with life belt (**Cherry**)
Basket of logs (**Stella**)
Wellingtons and towel (**Stella**)
Wine, two glasses and corkscrew (**Stella**)
Large towel (**Stella**)

| *Personal:* | **Stella:** glasses |
| | **Evan:** watch |

ACT II

SCENE 1

Strike:	**Evan**'s painting materials
Set:	**Evan**'s shoes
	Stella's glasses
Off stage:	Tray (**Mrs Tucket**)
	Socks (**Evan**)
	Bowl of grapes (**Stella**)
	Telegram (**Cherry**)
	Walking-stick (**Jimmy**)
Personal:	**Jimmy:** bandage

SCENE 2

Set:	Glass of beer (**Jimmy**)
	Telegram
Off stage:	Beer and glasses (**Stella**)
	Stella's glasses (**Evan**)
	Canvas (Stella's portrait) (**Evan**)
	Suitcase and suit jacket (**Evan**)

LIGHTING PLOT

Practical fittings required: storm lanterns, stove
Interior

ACT I, SCENE 1
To open: Full room lighting

Cue 1   **Stella** exits L with dinner-napkins   (Page 21)
            Lighting change for scene cross-over

ACT I, SCENE 2
To open: Cross-fade to indicate time change. Light fading and long
             shadow effect

Cue 2   **Stella**: " ... as wet as you say ..."   (Page 31)
            Lightning flash to accompany thunder

Cue 3   **Evan** exits to the harbour   (Page 33)
            Lightning flash to accompany thunder

Cue 4   **Stella** lights fire   (Page 33)
            Glow of light for stove effect

Cue 5   **Stella** re-enters room with towel   (Page 39)
            *Lights flicker on and off with thunder, then fail
             completely — leaving the stage in near-darkness*

Cue 6   **Stella** lights the storm lanterns   (Page 39)
            Dim light fills the room

Cue 7   **Stella** turns out to the harbour   (Page 40)
            The lights dim

Cue 8   **Evan** replaces the receiver   (Page 40)
            Black-out

ACT II, Scene 1

| *To open:* | Half-light morning effect. Rise to full room lighting, with bright sunshine outside, as scene progresses | |

| *Cue* 9 | **Evan** writes **Stella**'s telegram message | (Page 52) |
| | *Black-out* | |

| *Cue* 10 | Jazz recording plays | (Page 52) |
| | *Bring up room lighting on scene cross-over* | |

| *Cue* 11 | **Mrs Tucket** collects **Cherry**'s teacup and exits, L | (Page 52) |
| | *Fade to black-out* | |

ACT II, Scene 2

| *To open:* | Full room lighting | |

| *Cue* 12 | **Evan** throws the canvas into the stove | (Page 59) |
| | *Flicker of light from the stove* | |

| *Cue* 13 | **Jimmy**: "What are you doing, darling?" | (Page 65) |
| | *Start fade down to a solo spot on Stella* | |

| *Cue* 14 | **Stella**: " ... it'll reach the other side." | (Page 65) |
| | *Reduce to a pool of light around Stella, then begin fade* | |

| *Cue* 15 | **Stella** crumples the note in her hand | (Page 65) |
| | *Fade to black-out* | |

EFFECTS PLOT

Throughout the play the screech of gulls and the wash of the tide can be heard

ACT I

Scene 1

Cue 1	**Robert** looks out of the window *Ferry horn*	(Page 2)
Cue 2	**Mrs Tucket** exits, R *Increase sound of gulls and wash*	(Page 3)
Cue 3	**Cherry** and **Stella** exit, L *Ferry horn*	(Page 13)
Cue 4	**Cherry** looks out downstage *Ferry horn*	(Page 18)
Cue 5	**Evan**: "They always do, like homing pigeons." *Dinner-gong*	(Page 21)
Cue 6	**Stella** exits, L, with dinner-napkins *Crossover to* Scene 2: *Satie piano music plays; fade* *when ready*	(Page 21)

Scene 2

Cue 7	**Stella**: "Bye! Have a good time!" *Front door slams*	(Page 28)
Cue 8	**Stella**: " ... as wet as you say ... " *Rumble of thunder to accompany lightning flash*	(Page 31)
Cue 9	**Evan** exits to the harbour *Deafening crack of thunder to accompany lightning flash*	(Page 33)

Cue 10	**Stella**: "Evan! Be careful!"	(Page 33)
	Sounds of thunder, wind and rain to continue until the	
	end of the act; use to heighten tension at key moments.	
	By p. 38 the storm is at its strongest	
Cue 11	**Stella** stares out into the storm after **Evan**	(Page 39)
	Enormous thunder crack	
Cue 12	**Stella** re-enters room with a towel	(Page 39)
	Another thunder crack	
Cue 13	**Evan** and **Stella** look at each other; possibly about to kiss	(Page 40)
	Telephone rings	
Cue 14	**Evan**: "The ferry isn't running any more tonight."	(Page 40)
	Final rumble of thunder	

ACT II

SCENE 1

To open:	Satie piano music plays; fade when ready	
Cue 15	**Evan**: " ... marry **Robert**? Can you?"	(Page 51)
	Doorbell rings	
Cue 16	The Lights snap to black-out on SCENE 1	(Page 52)
	Traditional jazz recording plays; fade when ready	

SCENE 2

To open:	On stage radio plays at full blast	
Cue 17	**Stella** turns the radio off	(Page 53)
	Radio sound ceases	
Cue 18	**Jimmy** turns the radio back on	(Page 56)
	Radio sound at full blast	
Cue 19	**Jimmy**: "Christ! What's up with her?"	(Page 56)
	Radio sound down to a lower level as Cherry turns knob	

CPSIA information can be obtained
at www.ICGtesting.com
Printed in the USA
BVHW040316190920
589194BV00017B/1601

9 780573 019050